HOUSE of
WHITE
BIRCHES
PUBLISHERS
SINCE 1947

Easy Weekend
Afghans

Edited by Laura Scott

Easy Weekend Afghans

Copyright © 1999 House of White Birches, Berne, Indiana 46711

Editor: Laura Scott
Pattern Editor: Maggie Petsch Chasalow
Editorial Assistant: June Sprunger
Copy Editor: Mary Nowak
Editorial Coordinator: Tanya Turner

Photography: Tammy Christian, Jennifer Fourman, Jeff Chilcote
Photography Stylist: Arlou Wittwer
Photography Assistant: Linda Quinlan

Production Coordinator: Brenda Gallmeyer
Book Design: Sandy Bauman
Production Artist: Pam Gregory
Production Assistants: Shirley Blalock, Dana Brotherton, Carol Dailey
Traffic Coordinator: Sandra Beres

Publishers: Carl H. Muselman, Arthur K. Muselman
Chief Executive Officer: John Robinson
Marketing Director: Scott Moss
Product Development Director: Vivian Rothe
Publishing Services Manager: Brenda R. Wendling

Printed in the United States of America
First Printing: 1999
Library of Congress Number: 99-073196
ISBN: 1-882138-48-1

Every effort has been made to ensure the accuracy and completeness of the instructions in this book. However, we cannot be responsible for human error or for the results when using materials other than those specified in the instructions, or for variations in individual work.

Most of us today are pretty busy people. We have families to take care of and jobs that fill our days. Sometimes it may seem there is precious little time for our favorite hobby—crochet!

It is very often at the end of the day when the kids are in bed and the house is quiet and still that we are able to sit down on the sofa, turn on the television and pull out our current crochet project. Personally, I favor afghans because I can get into a steady rhythm as I work across each row. Yes, they take longer than some projects, but that makes it all the sweeter to finish one up!

This book takes into consideration your busy schedule, and your love of afghans. We've included more than 55 brand-new afghan patterns that can be crocheted from start to finish in just one weekend, roughly 16 hours or less. Granted, the actual time will depend on your crocheting speed and how much uninterrupted time you have. Rest assured, these afghans will not take months and months to finish.

As a treat to you, some of the afghans featured are crocheted with relatively new yarns on the market. A number of yarn companies, including Coats & Clark, Caron, Lion Brand and Spinrite, have worked hard to develop affordable yarns that are extra soft and/or textured and come in a rainbow of beautiful colors. I hope some of these yarns will inspire you to branch out and treat yourself to a gorgeous, yet inexpensive, yarn.

Whether you crochet these afghans as gifts for family and friends, to enter in the county fair, to give to charitable causes, or to snuggle up in with one of your children, I hope you find them to be a pleasure to crochet and share.

Warm regards,

Laura Scott

Editor, *Weekend Afghans*

Contents

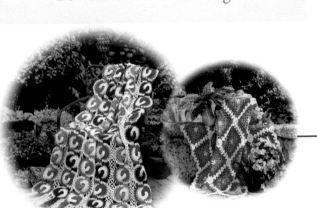

Eight-Hour Specials

*W*e all have times when
we need a special gift in a hurry!
This collection of seven beautiful
afghans is unique in that each afghan
can be made in only eight hours or
less—perfect for all those last-minute
gift-giving occasions, or simply for
any occasion at all!

Chapter 1

Hues of Rose & Blue

Design by Christina McNeese

If you enjoy adding warm and friendly country touches to your home, then this afghan worked in soft rose, blue and white will fit right in! Or, select coordinating colors to match your favorite armchair or loveseat.

Skill Level
Intermediate

Size
45" x 55" not including fringe

Materials
- Red Heart Super Saver worsted weight yarn (6 oz per skein): 5 skeins country rose #374 and 4 skeins each country blue #382 and white #311
- Size K/10½ crochet hook or size needed to obtain gauge

Gauge
3 dc = 2" with 2 strands held tog

Check gauge to save time.

Pattern Note
Afghan is worked with 2 strands held tog throughout.

Pattern Stitch
Fptr cl: Holding back on hook last lp of each st, fptr over st on row before last directly below st just worked, fptr over each of next 2 sts on row before last, yo, draw through all 4 lps on hook.

Afghan
Row 1 (RS): With white, ch 68 for foundation ch, ch 3 more for turning ch-3 (counts as first dc), dc in 4th ch from hook, dc in each rem ch across, ch 1, turn. (69 dc)

Row 2: Sc in each st across, sc in 3rd ch of turning ch-3, fasten off. (69 sc)

Row 3: With RS facing, attach country rose with a sl st in first sc, ch 3 (counts as first dc throughout), dc in each of next 5 sts, *fptr cl, sk next st on working row directly behind fptr cl just worked **, dc in each of next 7 sts, rep from * across, ending last rep at **, dc in each of last 6 sts, ch 1, turn.

Row 4: Rep Row 2.

Rows 5 & 6: With country blue, rep Rows 3 and 4.

Rows 7 & 8: With white, rep Rows 3 and 4.

Rows 9–68: Rep Rows 3–8 alternately; at end of Row 68, fasten off.

Finishing
Fringe
Cut 20 (13") strands country rose. Holding all 20 strands tog, fold strands in half, insert hook from WS to RS in first st on either short edge of afghan, draw folded end of strands through st to form a lp, draw free ends through lp, pull to tighten. Work 9 more fringes evenly sp across same edge. Rep on opposite short edge of afghan. ❖

Autumn Splendor

Design by Judy Teague Treece

*Capture the breathtaking beauty of a
New England autumn with this very easy afghan.
A simple pattern with basic color changes
makes this afghan perfect for beginning crocheters.*

Pattern Note

Join rnds with a sl st unless otherwise stated.

Afghan is worked with 2 strands held tog throughout.

Pattern Stitches

Shell: [3 dc, ch 2, 3 dc] in indicated sp.

Beg shell: [Ch 3, 2 dc, ch 2, 3 dc] in indicated sp.

Afghan

Rnd 1 (RS): With gold, ch 13, 2 dc in 4th ch from hook, ch 1, sk 2 chs, [3 dc in next ch, ch 1, sk 2 chs] twice, [{3 dc, ch 2} twice, 3 dc] in last ch; working in rem lps across opposite side of foundation ch, [ch 1, sk 2 chs, 3 dc in next ch] twice, ch 1, [3 dc, ch 2] twice in last ch, join in 3rd ch of beg ch-3, fasten off. (10 3-dc groups, counting last 3 chs of foundation ch as first dc)

Rnd 2: With RS facing, attach true rust with a sl st in last ch-2 sp worked, beg shell in same sp, *ch 1, [3 dc in next ch-1 sp, ch 1] rep across to next corner ch-2 sp, shell in corner ch-2 sp, ch 1 **, shell in next corner ch 2-sp, rep from * around, ending last rep at **, join in 3rd ch of beg ch-3.

Rnd 3: Sl st in each of next 2 dc and in next sp, beg shell in same sp, ch 1, [3 dc in next ch-1 sp, ch 1] rep across to next shell sp **, shell in shell sp, rep from * around, ending last rep at **, join in 3rd ch of beg ch-3 sp.

Rnd 4: Rep Rnd 3; fasten off.

Rnd 5: With RS facing, attach burgundy with a sl st in any corner shell sp, beg shell in same sp, *ch 1, [3 dc in next ch-1 sp, ch 1] rep across to next shell sp **, shell in next shell sp, rep from * around, ending last rep at **, join in 3rd ch of beg ch-3.

Rnds 6 & 7: Rep Rnds 3 and 4.

Rnds 8–10: With claret, rep Rnds 5–7.

Rnds 11–13: With true rust, rep Rnds 5–7.

Rnds 14–28: Rep Rnds 5–13 alternately, ending with a Rnd 10; at end of Rnd 28, do not fasten off.

Border

Ch 1, [sc, ch 2, sc] in same st as joining, ch 1, sk next dc, [sc, ch 2, sc] in next dc, ch 1, **[sc, ch 2, sc] in corner sp, *ch 1, [sc, ch 2, sc] in first dc of next 3-dc group, ch 1, sk next dc, [sc, ch 2, sc] in next dc of same 3-dc group, rep from * across to next corner, rep from ** around, ending with ch 1, join in beg sc, fasten off. ❖

Skill Level

Beginner

Size

Approximately 49" x 54"

Materials

- Red Heart Super Saver worsted weight yarn (8 oz per skein): 3 skeins claret #378, 2 skeins each true rust #285 and burgundy #376 and small amount honey gold #645
- Size N/15 crochet hook or size needed to obtain gauge

Gauge

Rnd 1 = 7½" x 2½" with 2 strands held tog

Check gauge to save time.

Midnight Wrapsody

Design by Beverly Forman

You'll treasure spending those quiet and peaceful nighttime hours curled up in this handsome afghan while reading a favorite book.

Pattern Note

Afghan is worked holding 2 strands tog throughout.

Pattern Stitch

Shell: [2 tr, ch 2, 2 tr] in indicated sp.

MC Panel (make 7)

Row 1 (RS): With MC, ch 8, join with sl st to form a ring, ch 4 (counts as first tr throughout), [shell, tr] in ring, turn.

Row 2: Ch 4, shell in shell sp, tr between last tr of shell and ch-4, turn.

Rows 3–31: Rep Row 2; at end of Row 31, fasten off.

First Joining Panel

Row 1: With RS facing, placing any 2 MC panels side by side so first row of one panel is directly across from last row of 2nd panel, attach CC with a sl st over end st of last row of first MC panel; working over ends of rows across, ch 1, sc over same st, ch 4, sc over end st of last row of 2nd MC panel, ch 5, sc over end st of next row on first MC panel, *ch 5, sk next row on 2nd MC panel, sc over end st of next row on 2nd MC panel**, ch 5, sk next row on first MC panel, sc over end st of next row on first MC panel, rep from * across, ending last rep at **, turn.

Skill Level

Intermediate

Size

Approximately 48" x 58" not including fringe

Materials

- Lion Brand Homespun worsted weight yarn (6 oz per skein): 6 skeins colonial #302 (MC) and 3 skeins Williamsburg blue #321 (CC)
- Size P/16 crochet hook or size needed to obtain gauge

Gauge

2 tr = 1⅛" with 2 strands held tog
Check gauge to save time.

Row 2: Ch 4, sc over first unworked end st on first row end of first MC panel, ch 4, sc over next unworked end st on next row of 2nd panel, *ch 5, sc over next unworked end st on first panel, ch 5, sc over next unworked end st on 2nd panel, rep from * across, ending with ch 5, sl st in beg sc, fasten off.

Rem 5 Joining Panels

Rows 1 & 2: Rep Rows 1 and 2 of first joining panel until all 7 MC panels have been joined.

Joining Panel Surface Ch

With RS facing, attach MC with a sl st over ch-4 sp at beg of first joining panel, ch 1, sc in same place, [ch 5, sc over Row 1 and Row 2 chs tog at point where chs cross] rep across to opposite end, ending with ch 4, sc over ch-4 sp at end of first joining panel, fasten off.

Rep on each of 5 rem joining panels.

Border

Attach CC with a sl st over end st of MC panel at right-hand edge of either short edge, ch 1, sc over same st, ch 5, sc in shell sp of same panel, *ch 5, sc over sp on first half of joining panel before surface ch, ch 5, sc over sp on 2nd half of same joining panel after surface ch, ch 5, sc in shell sp on next panel, rep from * across to corner, ch 5, sc over end st of same row, [ch 5, sk next row, sc over end st of next row] rep across to next corner, ch 5, sc in first shell sp across next short edge, rep from * around, ending with ch 5, join in beg sc, fasten off.

Finishing
Fringe

Cut 6 (12") lengths of CC for each ch-5 sp across each short end of afghan. Holding all 6 strands tog, fold strands in half, insert hook from WS to RS in first ch-5 sp on either short end, draw folded end through sp to form lp, draw free ends through lp, pull to tighten. Rep for each ch-5 sp across each short end. ❖

Bold Stripes Afghan

Design by Carolyn Christmas

Make a striking statement in your living or family room with this eye-catching, black afghan accented with bold fuschia and turquoise.

Skill Level
Intermediate

Size
Approximately 46" x 60" not including fringe

Materials
- Worsted weight yarn: 24 oz black and 12 oz each fuchsia and turquoise
- Size P/16 crochet hook or size needed to obtain gauge

Gauge
6 sts = 4" in pattern st with 2 strands held tog

Check gauge to save time.

Pattern Notes
Afghan is worked vertically, holding 2 strands tog throughout.

When beg and ending rows, leave approximately 10" ends to be worked into fringe.

Afghan
Row 1 (RS): With black, ch 133 for foundation ch, ch 3 more for turning ch (counts as first dc), 2 dc in 5th ch from hook, [sk 2 chs, 2 dc in next ch] rep across to last 2 chs, sk next ch, dc in last ch, turn. (44 dc pairs; 1 dc at each edge)

Row 2: Ch 3 (counts as first dc throughout), [2 dc between 2 dc of next dc pair] rep across, ending with dc in 3rd ch of turning ch-3, fasten off, turn. (44 dc pairs; 1 dc at each edge)

Row 3: Attach fuchsia with a sl st in first dc, ch 3, [2 dc between 2 dc of next dc pair] rep across, ending with dc in 3rd ch of turning ch-3, turn.

Row 4: Rep Row 2.

Rows 5 & 6: With black, rep Rows 3 and 4.

Rows 7 & 8: With turquoise, rep Rows 3 and 4.

Rows 9 & 10: With black, rep Rows 3 and 4.

Rows 11–46: Rep Rows 3–10 alternately, ending with Row 6.

Finishing
Fringe

Cut 4 (16") lengths of matching color for each row end. Holding all 4 strands tog, fold strands in half, insert hook from WS to RS over first row end st on either short edge of afghan, draw folded end of strand through st to form a lp, draw free ends through lp, pull to tighten. Rep with matching colors over end st of each row on both short ends of afghan. ❖

Oriental Spice

Design by Debby Caldwell

Whether worked in warm spice colors or muted pastels, this gorgeous afghan will add a decorator touch to your home.

Skill Level

Intermediate

Size

Approximately 40" x 57" excluding fringe

Materials

- Bernat Caress mohair-like worsted weight yarn (2.5 oz per skein): 21 skeins orient spice (foreground) #6200 or fruit mix (background) #6220
- Size M crochet hook or size needed to obtain gauge

Gauge

Cl shell = 2" with 2 strands held tog

Check gauge to save time.

Pattern Note

Afghan is worked holding 2 strands tog throughout.

Pattern Stitches

Cl: Holding back on hook last lp of each st, 2 tr in indicated st or sp, yo, draw through all 3 lps on hook.

Beg cl: [Ch 3, tr] in indicated st or sp.

Cl shell: [Cl, ch 3, cl] in indicated st or sp.

Beg cl shell: [Beg cl, ch 3, cl] in indicated st or sp.

Afghan

Row 1 (WS): Ch 98, sc in 2nd ch from hook and in each rem ch across, turn. (97 sc)

Row 2: Beg cl shell in first st, [ch 1, sk next 5 sc, cl shell in next sc] rep across, turn. (17 cl shells)

Row 3: Beg cl in first st, [ch 1, cl shell in next ch-1 sp] rep across, ending with ch 1, cl in last st of last cl, turn. (16 cl shells; 1 cl at each end)

Row 4: [Sl st, beg cl shell] in first ch-1 sp, [ch 1, cl shell in next ch-1 sp] rep across, turn. (17 cl shells)

Rows 5–48: Rep Rows 3 and 4 alternately; at end of Row 48, ch 1, turn.

Row 49: Sc in each cl, 3 sc in each ch-3 sp, and sc in each ch-1 sp across, fasten off.

Finishing

Fringe

Cut 6 (14)" lengths of yarn. Holding all 6 strands tog, fold strands in half, insert hook from WS to RS in end st on either short edge of afghan, draw folded end of strands through st to form a lp, draw free ends through lp, pull to tighten. Rep in every other st across same edge. Rep on opposite short edge. ❖

Quick & Cozy Afghan

Design by Holly Daniels

This attractive afghan makes a wonderful last-minute Christmas gift. Keep it in mind this year as a special gift for a special someone!

Pattern Notes

Afghan is worked holding 2 strands tog throughout.

Join rnds with a sl st unless otherwise stated.

Pattern Stitch

V-st: [Dc, ch 1, dc] in indicated st or sp.

Panel A (make 2)

Row 1 (RS): With A, ch 10 for foundation ch, ch 3 more for turning ch-3 (counts as first dc), dc in 4th ch from hook, dc in each rem ch across, turn. (11 dc)

Row 2: Ch 3 (counts as first dc throughout), working in back lps only this row, dc in each dc across, dc in 3rd ch of turning ch-3, turn. (11 dc)

Row 3: Ch 3, working in front lps only this row, dc in each dc across, dc in 3rd ch of turning ch-3, turn. (11 dc)

Rows 4–43: Rep Rows 2 and 3 alter-

Skill Level

Intermediate

Size

Approximately 50" x 52"

Materials

- Lion Brand Homespun worsted weight yarn (6 oz per skein): 6 skeins each colonial #302 (A) and mission #303 (B)
- Size Q crochet hook or size needed to obtain guage

Gauge

7 dc = 6" with 2 strands held tog
Check gauge to save time.

nately; at end of Row 43, do not fasten off, do not turn.

Border for Panel A

Rnd 1: Ch 3 (counts as first hdc, ch-1); working over ends of rows across long edge, *hdc evenly sp across to next corner **, [hdc, ch 1, hdc] in corner st, rep from * around, ending last rep at **, join in 2nd ch of beg ch-3, fasten off.

Panel B (make 3)

Row 1 (RS): With B, ch 9 for foundation ch, ch 3 more for turning ch-3 (counts as first dc), dc in 4th ch from hook, dc in each rem ch across, turn. (10 dc)

Row 2: Ch 3 (counts as first dc throughout), V-st in next dc, [sk next dc, V-st in next dc] 3 times, sk next dc, dc in 3rd ch of turning ch-3, turn. (4 V-sts)

Row 3: Ch 3, [V-st in next V-st sp] rep across, dc in 3rd ch of turning ch-3, turn. (4 V-sts)

Rows 4–38: Rep Row 3.

Row 39: Ch 3, dc in each rem dc across, fasten off. (10 dc)

Border for Panel B

Rnd 1: With RS facing, attach A with a sl st in last st of Row 39, rep Rnd 1 of border for Panel A, having same number of hdc on each side as on corresponding side of Panel A.

Assembly

With WS facing, beg with Panel B and alternating Panels B and A across, sc panels tog across long edges. ❖

Hearth & Home

Design by Ruth G. Shepherd

With its classic design and off-white color, this handsome afghan will suit any room and decor, from contemporary to Victorian.

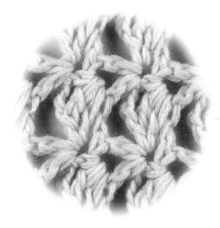

Skill Level
Intermediate

Size
Approximately 43" x 55" including edging

Materials
- Worsted weight yarn: 34 oz fisherman
- Size N/15 crochet hook or size needed to obtain gauge

Gauge
Ch 3, 2 dc in 3rd ch from hook, [ch 4, 2 dc in 3rd ch from hook] twice = 5" with 2 strands held tog

Check gauge to save time.

Pattern Note
Afghan is worked holding 2 strands held tog throughout.

Pattern Stitch
V-st: [Dc, ch 1, dc] in indicated st or sp.

Afghan
Row 1: Ch 10, sc in 7th ch from hook, ch 3, sc in last ch of ch-10, ch 3, 2 dc in 3rd ch from hook, [ch 4, 2 dc in 3rd ch from hook] 29 times, turn. (30 dc groups)

Row 2 (RS): Ch 10, sc in 7th ch from hook, ch 3, V-st in last ch of ch-10, ch 1, [V-st in ch-1 between next 2 dc groups, ch 1] 29 times, V-st in next sc, turn. (31 V-sts)

Row 3: Ch 10, sc in 7th ch from hook, ch 3, [sc, ch 3, 2 dc] in next V-st sp] 30 times, sc in last V-st sp, turn. (30 dc groups)

Row 4: Ch 10, sc in 7th ch from hook, ch 3, V-st in next sc, [ch 1, V-st in next sc] rep across, turn. (31 V-sts)

Rows 5–53: Rep Rows 3 and 4 alternately, ending with a Row 3; at end of Row 53, fasten off.

Edging
With RS facing, attach yarn with a sl st over first ch-3 sp at right-hand edge of either short edge of afghan, ch 1, sc in same st, *ch 4, [dc, ch 3, dc] in ch-6 sp at end of same row, ch 4, sc in next ch-3 sp at end of same row **, sc in ch-3 sp at end of next row, rep from * across, ending last rep at **, fasten off. Rep across opposite short edge. ❖

Summer Breezes

*A*s the sun sets after a warm, summer day, you'll enjoy wrapping up in any of these breezy summer afghans. With their open patterns and summery colors, they're just right for keeping out the cool air while adding a colorful touch to your decor.

Chapter 2

Friendship Rings

Design by Dot Drake

Express your affection for a treasured friend or family member with this enchanting afghan. Friendship rings will express your constant devotion and loyalty.

Pattern Note

Join rnds with a sl st unless otherwise stated.

Pattern Stitches

Picot (p): Ch 3, sc in top of dc just worked.

Joining p: Ch 1, sc in corresponding p on previous motif, ch 1, sc in last dc worked on working motif.

Joined tr (jtr): Holding back on hook last lp of each st, tr in next p on working motif, sk next free p on next motif, tr in next p, yo, draw through all lps on hook.

Panel A (make 3)
First Motif, First Circle

Rnd 1 (RS): Beg at top of panel, with MC, ch 15, join to form a ring, ch 3 (counts as first dc throughout), 30 dc in ring, join in 3rd ch of beg ch-3. (31 dc)

Rnd 2: Ch 4 (counts as first dc, ch-1 throughout), [dc in next dc, ch 1] 15 times, leave rem of rnd unworked; set aside.

First Motif, 2nd Circle

Rnd 1: With B, ch 15, draw first ch of ch-15 through center of Rnd 1 of first circle, join to form a ring, rep Rnd 1 of first circle.

Rnd 2: Rep Rnd 2 of first circle, do not set aside; dc in first ch-1 sp on Rnd 2 of first circle, [p, dc in next ch-1 sp] 14 times, drop B; pick up MC, dc in first ch-1 sp on Rnd 2 of 2nd circle, [p,

Skill Level
Intermediate

Size
Approximately 42" x 62" not including fringe

Materials
- Red Heart Super Saver worsted weight yarn (8 oz per skein): 3 skeins soft white #316 (MC), and 1 skein each mint #366 (A), raspberry #375 (B), light raspberry #774 (C) and dark teal #352 (D)
- Size G/6 crochet hook or size needed to obtain gauge

Gauge
Rnd 1 of first circle of first motif = 2¾" in diameter

Check gauge to save time.

dc in next ch-1 sp] 14 times, p, sc in next sp, fasten off MC; pick up B, p, sc in next sp, fasten off.

2nd Motif, First Circle

Rnds 1 & 2: Rep Rnds 1 and 2 of first circle of first motif.

2nd Motif, 2nd Circle

Rnd 1: With D, rep Rnd 1 of 2nd circle of first motif.

Rnd 2: Rep Rnd 2 of 2nd circle of first motif, replacing first 3 CC pcs of 2nd circle with joining ps to corresponding MC ps at bottom of previous motif and last 3 MC ps at top of 2nd motif to corresponding CC ps at bottom of previous motif. MC circle on MC and B

motif will be at right-hand side; MC circle on MC and D motif will be at left-hand side.

Rem 10 Motifs of Panel A

Alternating MC and B motifs with MC and D motifs and alternating placement of MC circles from right-hand side to left-hand side when joining each motif, make and join 10 more motifs as for 2nd motif.

Panel B (make 3)

Rep instructions for Panel A, beg with a MC and A motif and alternating with MC and C motifs, placing MC circle at left-hand edge for all MC and A motifs and at right-hand edge for all MC and C motifs when joining motifs, until 12 motifs have been joined.

Joining Panels

Row 1: With RS facing, attach MC with a sl st in 4th MC, p from bottom center of any Panel A, ch 4 (counts as first tr), dc in next p, [ch 3, sc in next p] 5 times, *ch 5, jtr, ch 5, sc in next p, [ch 3, sc in next p] 4 times, rep from * across, ending with ch 3; holding back on hook last lp of each st, dc in next p, tr in next p, fasten off.

Row 2: With RS facing, attach MC with a sl st in 4th CC p from top center of any Panel B, rep Row 1, do not fasten off.

Row 3: Ch 3, sl st in 4th ch of beg ch-4 on Row 1, sc in next sp on same panel, [ch 2, sc in next ch-3 sp on opposite panel] 9 times, *[ch 3, sc in next ch-5 sp on opposite panel] 4 times, ch 3, sc in next ch-3 sp on opposite panel, [ch 2, sc in next ch-3 sp on opposite panel] 7

Continued on page 40

Colors of Summer

Design by Melissa Leapman

Vibrant hues of red, blue, yellow and green make this textured cotton afghan perfect for cool summer evenings!

Skill Level

Intermediate

Size

Approximately 47" x 65" excluding fringe

Materials

- Lily Sugar 'n Cream sport worsted weight cotton by Spinrite (2½ oz per ball): 10 balls white #01 (A) and 6 balls each delft blue #28 (B), red #95 (C), yellow #10 (D) and verde green #53 (E)
- Size N/15 crochet hook or size needed to obtain gauge

Gauge

3-dc group = 1½" in pattern st with 2 strands held tog

Check gauge to save time.

Pattern Notes

Afghan is worked holding 2 strands tog throughout.

To change color in dc, work last dc before color change until last 2 lps before final yo rem on hook, drop working color to WS, yo with next color, complete dc.

Pattern Stitch

Long dc: Dc in next sp on row before last, drawing st up to top of working row.

Afghan

Row 1 (RS): With A, ch 94 (foundation ch), ch 4 more (turning ch-4), dc in 6th ch from hook, dc in each of next 2 chs, [ch 1, sk next ch, dc in each of next 3 chs] rep across to last 2 chs, ch 1, sk next ch, dc in last ch, turn. (23 3-dc groups; 1 dc at each edge, counting turning ch-4 as first dc, ch-1)

Row 2: Ch 4 (counts as first dc, ch-1), [sk next sp, dc in each of next 3 dc, ch 1] rep across to last 3-dc group, sk next ch of turning ch-4, dc in next ch, changing to B, fasten off A, turn. (23 3-dc groups; 1 dc at each edge)

Row 3: Ch 3 (counts as first dc throughout), long dc, dc in next dc, *ch 1, sk next dc, dc in next dc, long dc **, dc in next dc, rep from * across to last sp, ending last rep at **, dc in 3rd ch of turning ch-4, turn.

Row 4: Ch 3, dc in each of next 2 sts, [ch 1, sk ch-1 sp, dc in each of next 3 sts] rep across, ending with ch 1, dc in each of next 2 sts, dc in 3rd ch of turning ch-3, changing to C, fasten off B, turn.

Row 5: Ch 4, [sk next dc, dc in next dc, long dc, dc in next dc, ch 1] rep across to last 2 sts, sk next st, dc in 3rd ch of turning ch-3, turn.

Continued on page 40

Summer Delight

Design by Michele Wilcox

Imagine cheery yellow flowers against a clear blue sky as you crochet this delightfully easy afghan!

Pattern Notes

Afghan is worked with 2 strands held tog throughout.

Join rnds with a sl st unless otherwise stated.

Pattern Stitches

Shell: [3 dc, ch 2, 3 dc] in indicated sp or st.

Beg shell: [Ch 3, 2 dc, ch 2, 3 dc] in indicated sp or st.

Square (make 25)

Rnd 1 (RS): With yellow, ch 5, join to form a ring, ch 3 (counts as first dc throughout), [2 dc, ch 2, {3 dc, ch 2} 3 times] in ring, join in 3rd ch of beg ch-3, fasten off. (4 3-dc groups)

Rnd 2: With RS facing, attach light blue with a sl st in any corner ch-2 sp, beg shell in same sp, ch 1, [shell in next ch-2 sp, ch 1] rep around, join in 3rd ch of beg ch-3. (4 shells)

Rnd 3: Sl st in each of next 2 dc and in shell sp, beg shell in same sp, *ch 1, 3 dc in next ch-1 sp, ch 1 **, shell in next shell sp, rep from * around, ending last

Skill Level

Beginner

Size

Approximately 54½" square including border

Materials

- Lily Sugar 'n Cream worsted weight cotton yarn by Spinrite (110 yds per ball): 13 skeins delft blue #28, 12 skeins light blue #26, 10 skeins white #01 and 5 skeins yellow #10
- Size J/10 crochet hook or size needed to obtain gauge

Gauge

Rnds 1 and 2 of square = 4¼" square with 2 strands held tog

Check gauge to save time.

rep at **, join in 3rd ch of beg ch-3.

Rnd 4: Sl st in each of next 2 dc and in shell sp, beg shell in same sp, *ch 1, [3 dc in next ch-1 sp, ch 1] rep across to next shell **, shell in shell sp, rep from * around, ending last rep at **, join in 3rd ch of beg ch-3, fasten off.

Rnd 5: With RS facing, attach delft

blue with a sl st in any shell sp, beg shell in same sp, rep Rnd 4 from * around; do not fasten off.

Rnd 6: Rep Rnd 4.

Rnd 7: With white, rep Rnd 5; fasten off.

Assembly

Holding 2 squares with RS tog and working through both thicknesses at the same time, attach white with a sl st in any shell sp, ch 1, sc in same sp, *ch 3, [sc in next ch-1 sp, ch 3] rep across to next shell, sc in shell sp **; holding next 2 squares with RS tog and working through both thicknesses at the same time, sc in first shell sp on next 2 squares; rep from * across until 5 pairs of squares have been joined, ending last rep at **. Continue to join 5 more squares down next free side of piece already joined until all 25 squares have been joined, then rep across 4 unjoined edges running in opposite direction.

Border

With RS facing, attach yellow with a sl st in shell sp at any outside corner, ch 1, *[sc, 10 dc] in corner shell sp, [sc in next ch-1 sp, 7 dc in next ch-1 sp] rep across to next corner, treating sp between shells at each joining seam as ch-1 sp, rep from * around, join in beg sc, fasten off. ❖

CHAPTER 2

Pineapple Parfait

Design by Laura Gebhardt

If you enjoy the look of pineapple doilies, then you'll love the unique application of the classic pineapple motif in this pretty-as-a-picture afghan!

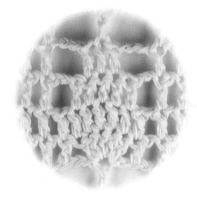

Skill Level
Intermediate

Size
Approximately 54" x 66"

Materials
- Worsted weight yarn: 48 oz pale yellow
- Size Q crochet hook or size needed to obtain gauge

Gauge
5 dc = 3¾" with 3 strands held tog
Check gauge to save time.

Pattern Notes
Afghan is worked with 3 strands held tog throughout.

Join rnds with a sl st unless otherwise stated.

Pattern Stitch
Picot (p): Ch 4, sl st in 3rd ch from hook.

Afghan
Row 1 (RS): Ch 82 for foundation ch, ch 4 more for turning ch (counts as first dc, ch-1), dc in 6th ch from hook, *sk 2 chs, 5 dc in next ch, sk 2 chs, dc in next ch **, [ch 1, sk next ch, dc in next ch] 3 times, rep from * across, ending last rep at **, ch 1, sk next ch, dc in last ch, turn. (7 5-dc groups)

Row 2: Ch 4 (counts as first dc, ch-1 throughout), *dc in each of next 7 dc, ch 1 **, [dc in next dc, ch 1] twice, rep from * across, ending last rep at **, dc in 3rd ch of turning ch-4, turn.

Row 3: Ch 5 (counts as first dc, ch-2 throughout), *sk next dc, dc in each of next 5 dc, ch 2, sk next dc **, dc in next dc, ch 1, dc in next dc, ch 2, rep from * across, ending last rep at **, dc in 3rd ch of turning ch-4, turn.

Row 4: Ch 6 (counts as first dc, ch-3 throughout), *sk ch-2 sp and next dc, dc in each of next 3 dc, ch 3, sk next dc and ch-2 sp **, dc in next dc, ch 1, dc in next dc, ch 3, rep from * across, ending last rep at **, dc in 3rd ch of turning ch-5, turn.

Row 5: Ch 7 (counts as first dc, ch-4 throughout), *dc in center dc of next 3-dc group, ch 4, sk next dc and ch-3 sp **, dc in next dc, ch 1, dc in next dc, ch 4, rep from * across, ending last rep at **, dc in 3rd ch of turning ch-6, turn.

Row 6: Ch 4, *sk 1 ch, dc in next ch, 5 dc in next ch, sk 2 chs, dc in next ch, ch 1 **, [dc in next dc, ch 1] twice, rep from * across, ending last rep at **, dc in 3rd ch of turning ch-7, turn.

Rows 7–45: Rep Rows 2–6 alternately, ending with a Row 5; do not fasten off at end of Row 45; ch 1, do not turn.

Continued on page 41

Snow White Afghan

Designed by Margret Willson

Soft and cuddly enough for a little princess, this pretty afghan looks like it just stepped out of a favorite fairy tale!

Pattern Note

Join rnds with a sl st unless otherwise stated.

Pattern Stitches

Shell: 5 dc in indicated st or sp.

V-st: [Dc, ch 1, dc] in indicated st or sp.

Afghan

Row 1 (RS): Ch 121 for foundation ch, ch 3 more for turning ch-3 (counts as first dc), 2 dc in 4th ch from hook, *sk 3 chs, V-st in next ch, sk 3 chs **, shell in next ch, rep from * across, ending last rep at **, 3 dc in last ch, turn. (15 V-sts, 14 shells, and 3 dc at each end)

Row 2: Ch 3 (counts as first dc throughout), dc in first st, [shell in next V-st sp, V-st in center dc of next shell] rep across to last V-st, shell in last V-st sp, 2 dc in 3rd ch of turning ch-3, turn.

Row 3: Ch 3, 2 dc in first st, [V-st in center dc of next shell, shell in next V-st sp] rep across to last shell, V-st in center dc of last shell, 3 dc in 3rd ch of turning ch-3, turn.

Rows 4–78: Rep Rows 2 and 3 alter-

Skill Level

Intermediate

Size

Approximately 42" x 60" including border

Materials

- Mohair-like worsted weight yarn: 30 oz white
- Size J/10 crochet hook or size needed to obtain gauge

Gauge

Shell = 1¾"

Check gauge to save time.

nately, ending with a Row 2; at end of Row 78, fasten off.

Border

Rnd 1: With RS facing, attach yarn with a sl st in top of end st at upper left-hand corner, ch 3, 8 dc in same st; †working over row ends across long edge, *dc dec over end sts of next 2 rows **, shell over end st of next row, rep from * across to next corner, ending last rep at **, 9 dc in corner st †; working across bottom, [dc dec over next 2 sps, shell at base of next shell] rep across to next corner, ending with

dc dec over next 2 sps, 9 dc in corner st; rep from † to †; working across top, [dc dec over 2nd and 4th dc of next shell, shell in next V-st sp] rep across to corner, ending with dc dec over 2nd and 4th dc of next shell, join in 3rd ch of beg ch-3.

Rnd 2: Sl st in next dc, ch 4 (counts as first dc, ch-1 throughout), [dc in next dc, ch 1] twice, **[{dc, ch 1} twice, dc] in next dc for corner, [ch 1, dc in next dc] 3 times, dc dec over next 2 dc, sk the dc dec between the 2 dc, *dc in next dc, ch 1, [{dc, ch 1} twice, dc] in next dc, ch 1, dc in next dc, dc dec over next 2 dc, sk the dc dec between the 2 dc, rep from * across to next corner, [dc in next dc, ch 1] 3 times, rep from ** around, ending with dc dec, join in 3rd ch of beg ch-4.

Rnds 3 & 4: Sl st in next ch and in next dc, ch 4, [dc in next dc, ch 1] twice, rep Rnd 2 from ** around.

Rnd 5: Sl st in next ch and next dc, ch 4, †[dc in next dc, ch 1] twice, 7 dc in next dc for corner, [ch 1, dc in next dc] 3 times, *dc dec over next 2 dc, sk the dc dec between the 2 dc, dc in next dc, ch 1 **, shell in next dc, ch 1, dc in next dc, rep from * across to next corner, ending last rep at **, rep from † around, ending with dc dec, join in 3rd ch of beg ch-4, fasten off. ❖

Spring Lilac Afghan

Design by Dot Drake

For a luxurious look and oh-so-soft feel without spending a fortune, crochet this lovely lilac-colored afghan in a faux mohair yarn!

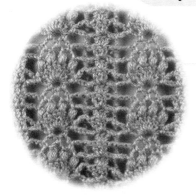

Pattern Stitches

Picot (p): Ch 3, sc in 3rd ch from hook.

Puff st: [Yo, draw up a lp] 3 times in indicated st, yo, draw through all lps on hook.

Afghan

Row 1: With smaller hook, p 71 times, ch 1, do not turn. (71 ps)

Row 2: Working into base of each p, 2 sc in each p across, turn. (142 sc)

Row 3 (RS): With larger hook, ch 3 (counts as first dc throughout), dc in each rem st across, turn. (142 dc)

Row 4: Ch 3, dc in each of next 4 sts, *ch 5, **sk next 4 sts, sc in next st, ch 3, sk next st, sc in next st, ch 5, sk 4 sts *, dc in next st †, ch 1, sk next st, 3 dc in next st, ch 1, sk next st, dc in next st, rep from * to *, dc in each of next 8 sts, ch 5, rep from ** across, ending last rep at †, dc in each of last 4 sts, turn.

Row 5: Ch 3, dc in each of next 4 dc, *ch 3, **sc in next ch-5 sp, ch 1, 7 dc in next ch-3 sp, ch 1, sc in next ch-5 sp, ch 3 *, fpdc over next dc, ch 1, 3 dc in center dc of next 3-dc group, ch 1, sk next dc, fpdc

Skill Level

Intermediate

Size

Approximately 42" x 52"

Materials

- Bernat Caress mohair-like worsted weight yarn (3 oz per skein): 5 skeins lilac
- Size F/5 crochet hook
- Size G/6 crochet hook or size needed to obtain gauge

Gauge

8 dc = 2½"with larger hook
Check gauge to save time.

over next dc, rep from * to *, dc in each of next 8 dc, ch 3, rep from ** across, ending with dc in each of last 5 dc, turn.

Row 6: Ch 3, dc in each of next 4 dc, *ch 3, **puff st in first dc of 7-dc group, [ch 3, sk next dc, puff st in next dc] 3 times, ch 3 *, bpdc over next fpdc, ch 1, 3 dc in center dc of next 3-dc group, ch 1, bpdc over next fpdc, rep from * to *, dc in each of next 8 dc, ch 3, rep from ** across, ending with dc in each of last 5 dc, turn.

Row 7: Ch 3, dc in each of next 4 dc, *ch 3, **sk next ch-3 sp, [sc in next ch-3 sp, ch 3] 3 times *, fpdc over next bpdc, ch 1, 3 dc in center dc of next 3-dc group, ch 1, fpdc over next bpdc, rep from * to *, dc in each of next 8 dc, ch 3, rep from ** across, ending with dc in each of last 5 dc, turn.

Row 8: Ch 3, dc in each of next 4 dc, *ch 5, **sk next ch-3 sp, sc in next ch-3 sp, ch 3, sc in next ch-3 sp, ch 5 *, bpdc over next fpdc, ch 1, 3 dc in center dc of next 3-dc group, ch 1, bpdc over next fpdc, rep from * to *, dc in each of next 8 dc, ch 5, rep from ** across, ending with dc in each of last 5 dc, turn.

Rows 9–95: Rep Rows 5–8 alternately, ending with a Row 7.

Row 96: Ch 3, dc in each of next 4 dc, *3 dc in next sp, **2 dc in next sp, dc in next sc, 2 dc in next sp, 3 dc in next sp *, dc in next fpdc, dc in each of next 3 dc, dc in next fpdc, rep from * to *, dc in each of next 8 dc, 3 dc in next sp, rep from ** across, ending with dc in each of last 5 dc, ch 1, turn. (142 dc)

Row 97: Sc in each dc across, turn. (142 sc)

Row 98: With smaller hook, [ch 3, hdc in 3rd ch from hook, sk next sc, sc in next sc] rep across, fasten off. ❖

Speedy Summer Stripes

Design by Melissa Leapman

You'll love how quickly and easily this pretty afghan works up! It's perfect for those busy, on-the-go weekends when you have just minutes here and there for crochet.

Pattern Notes

Afghan is worked from side to side with 2 strands held tog throughout.

When beg or ending a row, leave an 8" length for fringe.

Afghan

Row 1 (WS): With A, ch 136 (foundation ch), ch 3 more (turning ch-3), 2 dc in 5th ch from hook, [sk next ch, 2 dc in next ch] rep across to last 2 chs, sk next ch, dc in last ch, turn. (67 pairs of dc; 1 dc at each edge, counting turning ch-3 as first dc)

Row 2: Ch 3 (counts as first dc throughout), [2 dc between 2 dc of next dc pair] rep across to last dc pair, dc in 3rd ch of turning ch-3, fasten off, turn. (67 pairs of dc; 1 dc at each edge)

Row 3: Attach B with a sl st in top of first st, ch 3, [2 dc between 2 dc of next dc pair] rep across to last dc pair, dc in 3rd ch of turning ch-3, fasten off, turn.

Row 4: With C, rep Row 3.

Row 5: Rep Row 3.

Row 6: With A, rep Row 3, do not fasten off; turn.

Row 7: Rep Row 2.

Rep Rows 3–7 alternately until afghan measures approximately 40" or desired width, ending with a Row 7.

Skill Level

Intermediate

Size

Approximately 40" x 73" excluding fringe

Materials

- Lily Sugar 'n Cream worsted weight cotton by Spinrite (2½ oz per ball: 13 balls persimmon #33 (A), 11 balls white #01 (B) and 6 balls yellow #10 (C)
- Size N/15 crochet hook or size needed to obtain gauge

Gauge

1 dc pair = 1" in pattern st with 2 strands held tog

Check gauge to save time.

Finishing
Fringe

Cut 9 (16") lengths of A. Holding all 9 lengths tog, fold strands in half. Insert hook from WS to RS over end st of first row along either short edge of afghan, draw folded end of strands through to form a lp, draw free ends of strands through lp and pull to tighten. Matching color of yarn to row being worked, rep for each row across same edge and each row across opposite short edge. ❖

Designer Tips

Starting a New Color

Rather than tying on a new color, I fasten off the last color used and begin the new one by drawing up a loop in the specified stitch and then chaining the necessary number of stitches to begin the pattern round of the next row. It's faster than tying on a new color, the pattern is always sharper with no color bleed-through, and you will have the same number of ends to weave in.

— Katherine Eng

Mastering Motifs

When making a large batch of motifs for an afghan that has many color changes, I like to work all the centers first, then all of the next color pattern around each motif, etc., rather than working each complete motif separately. After working just a few in this manner, you will know the pattern stitch by heart and can work it without referring to notes or instructions. The work proceeds much faster.

— Katherine Eng

Save a Step

When working with blocks or motifs that will be sewn together later, leave a tail of yarn approximately twice the length of the seam to be sewn when fastening off. This will eliminate the need to tie on additional yarn for sewing and will result in fewer tails to work in.

— Darla J. Fanton

Triple Ripple Afghan

Design by Zelda Workman

*If you enjoy crocheting ripples, then this
lively afghan will give you
three times the fun with three times the ripples!*

Pattern Note

Afghan is worked with 2 strands held tog throughout.

End Panel (make 2)

Row 1 (RS): With lilac, ch 30 for foundation ch, ch 2 more for turning ch-2 (counts as first hdc), hdc in 4th ch from hook, hdc in each of next 12 chs, 3 hdc in next ch, hdc in each of next 13 chs, sk next ch, hdc in last ch, turn. (31 hdc)

Row 2: Ch 3 (counts as first dc throughout), sk next hdc, dc in next hdc, [ch 1, sk next hdc, dc in next hdc] 6 times, 3 dc in next hdc, dc in next hdc, [ch 1, sk next hdc, dc in next hdc] 6 times, sk next hdc, dc in 2nd ch of turning ch-2, turn.

Row 3: Ch 2 (counts as first hdc throughout), sk next dc, [hdc in next ch, hdc in next dc] 6 times, hdc in next dc, 3 hdc in next dc, hdc in next dc, [hdc in next dc, hdc in next ch] 6 times, sk next dc, hdc in 3rd ch of turning ch-3, fasten off lilac, turn.

Row 4: Attach white with a sl st in last st of last row, ch 2, sk next hdc, hdc in each of next 13 hdc, 3 hdc in next hdc, hdc in each of next 13 hdc, sk next hdc, hdc in 2nd ch of turning ch-2, turn.

Rows 5 & 6: Rep Rows 2 and 3; fasten off white at end of Row 6.

Row 7: With lilac, rep Row 4.

Skill Level

Beginner

Size

Approximately 47" x 66"

Materials

- Red Heart Super Saver worsted weight yarn (8 oz per skein): 4 skeins each white #311 and lilac #353
- Size P/16 crochet hook or size needed to obtain gauge
- Yarn needle

Gauge

End Panel = 15¾" wide with 2 strands held tog

Check gauge to save time.

Designer Tips

For Gift Afghans

When making an afghan for a gift, be sure to include a small card with the laundering instructions found on the yarn label.

— Darla J. Fanton

A Fine Finish for Ripple Afghans

Most ripple afghans call for "sc in back lp only" across. However, I've found that one way to obtain a great finished look is to work through both loops for 3 stitches at the beginning of each row, through back loop only across to end of each row, then through both loops of last 3 stitches. Instead of skipping that last stitch on

Rows 8 & 9: Rep Rows 5 and 6; fasten off lilac at end of Row 9.

Rows 10–54: Rep Rows 4–9 alternately, ending with a Row 6.

Center Panel

Rows 1–3: With white, rep Rows 1–3 of end panel.

Rows 4–6: With lilac, rep Rows 4–6 of end panel.

Rows 7–9: With white, rep Rows 7–9 of end panel.

Rows 10–54: Rep Rows 4–9 alternately, ending with a Row 6.

Finishing

With yarn needle, sew panels tog on the WS. ❖

each beginning and ending of rows that have to be skipped, sc the first 2 tog through both loops at beg, sc through both lps for 2 more sts, sc in back lp only in each st across to last 4 sts, sc in both lps for 2 sts, sc last 2 sts tog through both loops. This will greatly reinforce the sides to keep from stretching and will keep the life of the afghan for many years.

— Shirley Patterson

Keeping Your Place

A Post-It note is helpful as it is easily moved down the instructions to highlight the row you are working on. You can also use it to keep track of the number of repeats or make other notes.

— Darla J. Fanton

CHAPTER 2

Friendship Rings
Continued from page 24

times, rep from * across, ending with [ch 2, sc in next sp on opposite panel] 9 times, sl st in 4th ch of beg ch-4 on same panel, ch 3, sl st in last tr on opposite panel, fasten off.

Alternating Panels A and B, rep Rows 1–3 until all 6 panels have been joined.

Finishing

Matching colors to each p and ch-sp across both short ends of afghan, cut 3 (12") lengths of yarn for each p and ch-sp. Holding 3 strands tog, fold strands in half, insert hook from WS to RS in first st or sp, draw folded end of strand through st or sp to form a lp, draw free ends through lp, pull to tighten. Rep for each p and each sp across both short ends. ❖

Colors of Summer
Continued from page 26

Row 6: Ch 4, [sk next sp, dc in each of next 3 sts, ch 1] rep across, ending with

sk 4th ch of turning ch-4, dc in next ch, changing to D, fasten off C, turn.

Rows 7–82: Rep Rows 3–6 for pattern in the following color sequence, ending with a Row 6 in A: [2 rows D, 2 rows E, 2 rows A, 2 rows B, 2 rows C].

Finishing
Fringe

Cut 10 (12") lengths of A. Holding all 10 strands tog, fold in half. Insert hook from WS to RS through first ch-1 sp across either short edge of afghan, draw folded end of strands through sp to form a lp, draw loose ends of strands through lp, pull to tighten. Rep for each ch-1 sp across same edge and across opposite short edge. ❖

Pineapple Parfait
Continued from page 30

Border

[Sc, p, ch 1, sc] in last dc made; *working in end sts across side of afghan, [p, ch 1, sc in top of end st of next row] rep across to corner, ending with p, ch 1, [sc, p, ch 1, sc] in corner; [p, ch 1, sk 2 sts, sc in next st] rep across to next corner, ending with p, ch 1 **, [sc, p, ch 1, sc] in corner, rep from * around, ending last rep at **, join in beg sc, fasten off. ❖

Designer Tips

Add a Pocket

When making an afghan as a gift for a shut-in or someone in a nursing home, using matching yarn and hook, make a pocket about 6 inches square and sew it onto the back of the afghan. This makes a very handy place for tissue, hanky, keys, etc. Also, the yarn from the pocket can be used whenever a need arises for mending the afghan.

— Ruth G. Shepherd

Tip for Sore, Stiff Hands

When arthritis or sore hands become a problem, try wrapping the crochet hook with several layers of adhesive tape from the middle of the handle to the end of the stem. This will provide a better grip and a slightly softer surface for the fingers.

— Ruth G. Shepherd

Counting Tip

When making an afghan that requires many blocks or motifs, stack the pieces in groups of 10 as they are made and run a length of contrasting yarn through the center of each group, tying them together loosely. This helps eliminate the need to count and recount blocks as work progresses.

— Ruth G. Shepherd

Add a Sachet

If the afghan you are making is made from rather small powder decorative motifs, make two extra motifs, weave them together with a length of ribbon, stuffing with fiberfill and a bit of sachet before closing for a lovely sachet to keep the afghan sweet-smelling when stored.

— Ruth G. Shepherd

Party Fun

Entertaining 10- or 11-year-old girls at a birthday party can be a chore. Try making up small kits containing a size G crochet hook, a bit of yarn and a small, completed granny square. Offer to teach the girls how to make one of their own. Girls this age catch on very quickly and will soon be making a pillow, napkin, small afghan or tote bag of their own.

— Ruth G. Shepherd

Easy Storage

Store leftover skeins and scraps of yarn in clear zip-top bags, using a separate bag for each color. When ready to begin, you can easily decide which combination of colors you want to use by gathering the bags and arranging them side by side. You can easily rearrange the bags and the yarns will stay neat as you decide which shades to use.

— Isabelle Wolters

Take the Long View

When choosing colors, work up several swatches and look at them from a distance rather than close up, and preferably in the location where you plan to use the afghan. You will get a more realistic view of how the color combination will look and which combinations you prefer.

— Isabelle Wolters

Use Up Those Leftovers

When trying to use up leftover yarns of different weights for scrap afghans, combine two or more strands of a lighter weight yarn to achieve the weight of thicker yarns: 2 or more strands of baby yarn or sport weight to equal 1 strand of worsted weight, 2 strands of worsted—or 1 strand of worsted and 1 strand of sport—to equal 1 strand of bulky or chunky weight. Use similar colors or combine different colors for a tweedy effect. Be sure the care properties are the same (machine-washable and dryable).

— Isabelle Wolters

Fireside Warmers

*C*url up on those cool winter nights
with any of these attractive and
cozy afghans. As beautiful as they are
warm, they are designed to soothe you,
body and soul.

Chapter 3

Mexican Siesta

Design by Maggie Weldon

Spice up your decor with this zesty afghan featuring vibrant Mexican-blanket colors!

Pattern Notes

Join rnds with a sl st unless otherwise stated.

After working fptr, do not work into top of st on working row directly behind fptr.

Pattern Stitches

Shell: [2 dc, ch 2, 2 dc] in indicated st.

Beg shell: [Ch 3, dc, ch 2, 2 dc] in indicated st.

Afghan

Row 1 (RS): With MC, ch 118 (foundation ch), ch 3 more (turning ch-3), dc in 4th ch from hook and in each rem ch across, turn. (119 dc, counting turning ch-3 as first dc)

Row 2: Ch 3 (counts as first dc throughout), dc in each rem st across, fasten off. (119 dc)

Skill Level

Intermediate

Size

Approximately 50" x 58"

Materials

- Coats & Clark TLC worsted weight yarn (5 oz per skein): 3 skeins cognac #5288 (MC), and 2 skeins each dark sage #5666 (A), red #5900 (B), amber #5644 (C) and navy #5861 (D)
- Size N/15 crochet hook or size needed to obtain gauge

Gauge

5 dc = 2"

Check gauge to save time.

Row 3: With RS facing, attach A with a sl st in first st, ch 3, [fptr over next st in row before last, drawing st up to top of working row; dc in each of next 3 sts] rep across to last 2 sts, fptr over next st in row before last, dc in next st, turn. (119 sts)

Row 4: Rep Row 2.

Row 5: With RS facing, attach B with a sl st in first st, ch 3, dc in each of next 2 sts, [fptr over next st in row before last, drawing st up to top of working row; dc in each of next 3 sts] rep across, turn.

Row 6: Ch 3, dc in each rem st across, turn.

Row 7: Rep Row 2.

Rows 8 & 9: With C, rep Rows 3 and 4.

Rows 10–12: With D, rep Rows 5–7.

Row 13: With MC, rep Row 3.

Row 14: Rep Row 6.

Rows 15–92: Rep Rows 2–14 alternately 6 times; at end of Row 92, do not fasten off; turn.

Border

Beg shell in first st, dc in each st across to corner, shell in corner st, *working over ends of rows across, dc over end st of first row, 2 dc over end st of each row to last row, dc over end st of last row *, shell in first rem lp of foundation row, working in rem lps of foundation row, dc in each st across to last st, shell in last st, rep from * to *, join in 3rd ch of beg ch-3, fasten off. ❖

Spruce & Lace

Design by Maggie Weldon

The soft shades of green and off-white in this afghan will easily complement many decors.

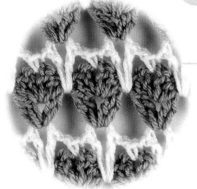

Pattern Note

Join rnds with a sl st unless otherwise stated.

Pattern Stitches

Shell: [2 dc, ch 1, 2 dc] in indicated st or sp.

V-st: [Dc, ch 2, dc] in indicated st or sp.

Afghan

Row 1 (RS): With MC, ch 118 (foundation ch), ch 3 more (turning ch-3), shell in 6th ch from hook, [sk 3 chs, shell in next ch] rep across to last 3 chs, sk 2 chs, dc in last ch, turn. (29 shells, 1 dc at each edge, counting turning ch-3 as first dc)

Row 2: Ch 3 (counts as first dc throughout), shell in each shell sp across, dc in 3rd ch of turning ch-3, fasten off, turn.

Row 3: With RS facing, attach CC with a sl st in first dc, ch 1, sc in same st, ch 1, sc in next shell sp, ch 1, [working over sts of last row, V-st between shell directly below same shell in which last sc was worked and next shell in row before last; ch 1, sc in next shell sp on last row, ch 1] rep across, sc in 3rd ch of turning ch-3, fasten off, do not turn.

Row 4: With RS facing, attach MC

Skill Level

Intermediate

Size

Approximately 56" x 60"

Materials

- Coats & Clark TLC worsted weight yarn (5 oz per skein): 9 skeins spruce #5662 (MC) and 4 skeins natural #5017 (CC)
- Size N/15 crochet hook or size needed to obtain gauge

Gauge

Shell = 2"

Check gauge to save time.

with a sl st in first sc, ch 3, 2 dc in same st, shell in each V-st sp across, 3 dc in last sc, turn. (28 shells, 1 dc at each edge, counting turning ch-3 as first dc)

Row 5: Ch 3, 2 dc in first st, shell in each shell sp across, 3 dc in 3rd ch of turning ch-3, fasten off, turn.

Row 6: With RS facing, attach CC with a sl st in first dc, ch 1, sc in same st, ch 1, working over sts of last row, V-st between last dc of 3-dc group directly below same 3-dc group in which last sc was worked and next shell in row before last, *ch 1, sc in next shell sp on last row, ch 1 **, working over sts of last row, V-st between shell directly below same shell in which last sc was

worked and next shell in row before last, rep from * across to last shell, ending last rep at **, working over sts of last row, V-st between shell directly below same shell in which last sc was worked and next 3-dc group in row before last, ch 1, sc in 3rd ch of turning ch-3, fasten off, do not turn.

Row 7: With RS facing, attach MC with a sl st in first sc, ch 3, shell in each V-st sp across, dc in last sc, turn. (29 shells, 1 dc at each edge)

Rows 8–95: Rep Rows 2–7, ending with a Row 5; do not fasten off at end of Row 95; turn.

Border

Rnd 1: Ch 3, [dc, ch 2, 2 dc] in first st, dc in each of next 2 dc, sk next dc, dc in next dc, [sk next ch-1 sp, dc in each of next 4 dc] rep across to next corner, [2 dc, ch 2, 2 dc] in 3rd ch of turning ch-3, *working over end sts of rows across, work an odd number of dc evenly sp across to next corner *, [2 dc, ch 2, 2 dc] in first rem lp of foundation ch; dc in each rem lp across foundation ch to last st, [2 dc, ch 2, 2 dc] in last st, rep from * to *, join in 3rd ch of beg ch-3, fasten off.

Rnd 2: With RS facing, attach CC with a sl st in any corner ch-2 sp, ch 1, beg in same sp, *[sc, ch 4, sc] in corner sp, ch 3, [sk next dc, sc in next dc, ch 3] rep across to next corner, rep from * around, join in beg sc, fasten off. ❖

Winter Stripes

Design by Maggie Weldon

Like the beauty of freshly fallen snow on a clear day, this lovely wintry afghan will soothe your body and soul.

Skill Level
Beginner

Size
Approximately 45" x 70" not including fringe

Materials
- Coats & Clark TLC worsted weight yarn (5 oz per skein): 6 skeins each white #5001 (A) and medium blue #5823 (B)
- Size N/15 crochet hook or size needed to obtain gauge

Gauge
6 shells = 7"

Check gauge to save time.

Pattern Note
Afghan is worked from side to side.

Pattern Stitch
Shell: [Sc, hdc, dc] in indicated st or sp.

Afghan
Row 1 (RS): With A, ch 182, shell in 2nd ch from hook, [sk 2 chs, shell in next ch] rep across to last 3 chs, sk next 2 chs, sc in last ch, ch 1, turn. (60 shells)

Row 2: Shell in first st, [shell in next sc] rep across to last sc, sc in last sc, fasten off, turn.

Row 3: With RS facing, attach B with a sl st in first st, ch 1, shell in first st, [shell in next sc] rep across to last sc, sc in last sc, ch 1, turn.

Row 4: Rep Row 2.

Row 5: With RS facing, attach A with a sl st in first st, ch 1, shell in first st, [shell in next sc] rep across to last sc, sc in last sc, ch 1, turn.

Row 6: Rep Row 2.

Rep Rows 3–6 until afghan measures approximately 45" or desired width, ending with a Row 6, fasten off.

Finishing
Fringe
Beg over end st of first row on either short edge and matching color of fringe to color of row being worked, cut 3 (10") lengths of yarn. Holding all 3 lengths tog, fold lengths in half, insert hook from WS to RS over end st of row, draw folded end through st to form a lp, draw free ends through lp and pull tightly. Continuing to match color of fringe to row being worked and working in every other row, rep across first short edge.

Rep on rem short edge. ❖

Perfectly Plaid

Design by Nazanin S. Fard

Crochet this unique afghan as a special lap throw for a friend or family member who enjoys curling up with an afghan in an armchair.

Pattern Note

Afghan is worked holding 2 strands tog throughout.

Afghan

Row 1 (RS): With A, ch 94 (foundation ch), ch 3 more (turning ch-3), dc in 4th ch from hook, dc in each of next 3 chs, [ch 1, sk next ch, dc in each of next 8 chs] rep across, turn. (85 dc, counting turning ch-3 as first dc; 10 ch-1 sps)

Row 2: Ch 3 (counts as first dc throughout), dc in each of next 7 dc, [ch 1, dc in each of next 8 dc] rep across to last 5 sts, ch 1, dc in each of next 4 dc, dc in 3rd ch of turning ch-3, turn.

Row 3: Ch 3, dc in each of next 4 dc, [ch 1, dc in each of next 8 dc] rep across, turn.

Row 4: Rep Row 2, fasten off, turn.

Row 5: With RS facing, attach C with a sl st in first st, ch 1, sc in same st and in each of next 4 dc, [ch 1, sc in each of next 8 dc] rep across, fasten off, turn.

Skill Level

Intermediate

Size

Approximately 42" x 45" excluding fringe

Materials

- Spinrite Bernat Caress worsted weight yarn (3 oz per skein): 7 skeins dusty rose #6144 (A), 6 skeins off-white #6104 (B) and 2 skeins navy #6107 (C)
- Size P/16 crochet hook or size needed to obtain gauge

Gauge

8 dc = 3³/₄" with 2 strands held tog

Check gauge to save time.

Row 6: With WS facing, attach B with a sl st in first sc, ch 3, dc in each of next 7 sc, [ch 1, dc in each of next 8 sc] rep across to last 5 sc, ch 1, dc in each of last 5 sc, turn.

Row 7: Rep Row 3.

Row 8: Rep Row 2.

Row 9: Rep Row 3, fasten off, turn.

Row 10: With WS facing, attach C with a sl st in first st, ch 1, sc in same st and in each of next 7 dc, [ch 1, sc in each of next 8 dc] rep across to last 5 sts, ch 1, sc in each of next 4 dc, sc in 3rd ch of turning ch-3, fasten off.

Row 11: With RS facing, attach A with a sl st in first sc, ch 3, dc in each of next 4 sc, [ch 1, dc in each of next 8 sc] rep across, turn.

Rows 12–64: Rep Rows 2–11 alternately, ending with a Row 4.

Finishing
Vertical Stripes

Beg at bottom of any column of ch-1 sps, with 2 strands C held tog, sl st in each sp to top of column, fasten off. Rep for each column across.

Fringe

Cut 2 (15") lengths of A. Holding both lengths tog, fold lengths in half, insert hook from WS to RS through first st along either short edge of afghan, pull folded end of strands through to form a lp, pull free ends through lp and tighten. Alternating A and B, rep for each st across edge. Rep across opposite short edge. ❖

Shades of Nature

Design by Maggie Weldon

*Shades of brown blend together to create
a lovely effect in this handsome afghan.*

Skill Level

Intermediate

Size

Approximately 40" x 62" including border

Materials

- Spinrite Berella "4" worsted weight yarn (3.5 oz per skein): 9 skeins oak #8796 (A), 6 skeins walnut #8916 (B) and 5 skeins honey #8795 (C)
- Size Q crochet hook or size needed to obtain gauge

Gauge

[Fpdc, bpdc] = 1" with 2 strands held tog

Check gauge to save time.

Pattern Notes

Afghan is worked holding 2 strands tog throughout.

Join rnds with a sl st unless otherwise stated.

Afghan

Row 1 (RS): With B, ch 70 (foundation ch), ch 3 more (turning ch-3), dc in 4th ch from hook and in each rem ch across, fasten off. (71 dc, counting turning ch-3 as first dc)

Row 2: With RS facing, attach A with a sl st in 3rd ch of turning ch-3, ch 2 (counts as first hdc throughout), fpdc over next st, [bpdc over next st, fpdc over next st] rep across to last st, hdc in last st, fasten off. (71 sts)

Row 3: With RS facing, attach C with a sl st in 2nd ch of turning ch-2, ch 2, fpdc over next st, [bpdc over next st, fpdc over next st] rep across to last st, hdc in last st, fasten off. (71 sts)

Rows 4–49: Rep Row 3 in the following color sequence, ending with B: [A, B, A, C].

Border

With RS facing, attach B with a sl st in upper right corner, ch 3, 2 dc in same st, dc in each rem st across to corner, *3 dc in corner st; working over ends of rows, dc evenly sp across to next corner *, 3 dc in corner st, dc in each rem lp of foundation ch across to next corner, rep from * to *, join in 3rd ch of beg ch-3, fasten off. ❖

Northern Lights

Design by Dot Drake

Anyone who has seen the Northern Lights knows it is a sight to remember for a lifetime. Capture the beauty of this natural wonder in this gorgeous afghan!

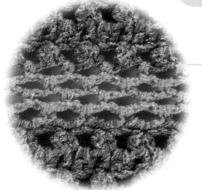

Pattern Note

Afghan is worked from side to side holding 3 strands tog throughout.

Pattern Stitches

Bobble: [Tr, sc] in indicated st, pushing bobble to RS of work.

Dc cl: Holding back on hook last lp of each st, 2 dc in indicated st or sp, yo, draw through all 3 lps on hook.

Beg dc cl: [Ch 2, dc] in indicated st or sp.

Afghan

Row 1 (RS): With 1 strand each of A, B, and C held tog, ch 173, sc in 2nd ch from hook and in each rem ch across, turn. (172 sc)

Row 2: Beg dc cl in first sc, [ch 2, sk 2 sc, bobble in next sc] rep across to last 3 sts, ch 2, sk 2 sc, dc cl in last sc, turn. (56 bobbles)

Row 3: Ch 3 (counts as first dc throughout), 2 dc in next sp, [dc in next sc, 2 dc in next sp] rep across to last sp, dc in beg dc cl, ch 1, turn. (172 dc)

Row 4: Sc in first st, [ch 2, sk 2 dc, bobble in next dc] rep across to last 3 sts, ch 2, sk 2 dc, sc in 3rd ch of turning

Skill Level

Intermediate

Size

43" x 72" excluding fringe

Materials

- Spinrite Bernat Coordinates sport-weight yarn (6 oz per skein): 6 skeins sailor blue #1019 (A), and 4 skeins each grape #1018 (B) and birds of paradise #1021 variegated (C)
- Size N/15 crochet hook or size needed to obtain gauge

Gauge

12 sc = 5" with 3 strands held tog
Check gauge to save time.

ch-3, turn. (56 bobbles)

Row 5: Ch 3, [2 dc in next sp, dc in next sc] rep across, turn. (172 dc)

Row 6: Rep Row 4.

Rows 7 & 8: Rep Rows 5 and 6; at end of Row 8, fasten off, turn.

Row 9: With RS facing, attach 3 strands A held tog with a sl st in first sc of last row, ch 3, dc in next sp, ch 3, [sc in next sp, ch 3] rep across to next-to-last sp, dc in last sp, dc in last sc, ch 1, turn. (56 sps)

Row 10: Sc in first dc, [ch 3, sc in next

sp] rep across to last sp, ch 3, sc in turning ch-3, turn. (57 sps)

Rows 11: Ch 3, dc in next sp, ch 3, [sc in next sp, ch 3] rep across to next-to-last sp, dc in last sp, dc in last sc, ch 1, turn. (56 sps)

Row 12: Rep Row 10; fasten off, turn.

Row 13: With RS facing, attach 1 strand each of A, B, and C with a sl st in first sc of last row, ch 1, sc in same st, 2 sc in next sp, 3 sc in each rem sp across, sc in last sc, turn. (172 sc)

Rows 14–24: Rep Rows 2–12.

Rows 25–68: Rep Rows 13–24 alternately, ending with a Row 8; do not fasten off at end of Row 68, ch 1, turn.

Row 69: Sc in each sc, 2 sc in each sp across, ch 1, turn.

Row 70: Sl st in each sc across, fasten off.

Finishing
Fringe

Cut 1 (14") strand each of A, B, and C. Holding all 3 strands tog, fold strands in half, insert hook from WS to RS in end st of first row on either short edge of afghan, draw folded end of strands through st to form lp, draw free ends of strands through lp and pull tightly. Work one 3-strand group over each sc end st and two 3-strand groups over each dc or dc cl end st across same short edge. Rep across opposite short edge of afghan. ❖

Celtic Cables

Design by Angela J. Tate

Crocheted with a large, size Q crochet hook, this warm afghan is reminiscent of classic Irish crochet.

Skill Level

Beginner

Size

Approximately 48" x 60" excluding fringe

Materials

- Coats & Clark Red Heart Super Saver worsted weight yarn (8 oz per skein): 10 skeins aran #313
- Size Q crochet hook or size needed to obtain gauge

Gauge

3 dc = 2" with 3 strands held tog.

Check gauge to save time.

Pattern Note

Afghan is worked from side to side, holding 3 strands tog throughout.

Afghan

Row 1 (RS): Ch 92, dc in 4th ch from hook and in each rem ch across, ch 1, turn. (90 dc, counting last 3 chs of foundation ch as first dc)

Row 2: Working in back lps only this row, sl st in each st across, turn.

Row 3: Ch 3 (counts as first dc throughout), working in rem lps of row before last, dc in each rem st across, ch 1, turn. (90 dc)

Rep Rows 2 and 3 until afghan measures approximately 48" or desired width, ending with a Row 2, fasten off.

Finishing

With RS facing, attach yarn with a sl st in first rem lp of foundation ch, sl st in each rem lp across, fasten off.

Fringe

Cut 10 (16") lengths of yarn. Holding all strands tog, fold strands in half. Insert hook from WS to RS over end st of first dc row on either short edge of afghan, pull folded end of strands through st on hook to form a lp, pull free ends through lp and tighten. Rep for each dc row across short edge. Rep on opposite short edge. ❖

Soft Circles

Design by Vicki Blizzard

Give your living room or bedroom an elegant, Victorian touch with this exquisite afghan.

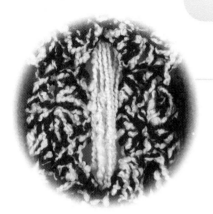

Pattern Note

Afghan is worked from side to side, holding 1 strand A and 1 strand B tog throughout.

Pattern Stitches

Shell: 5 dc in indicated st or sp.

Half shell: 3 dc in indicated st or sp.

Beg half shell: [Ch 3 (counts as first dc), 2 dc] in indicated st or sp.

Dc3tog: Holding back on hook last lp of each st, dc in each of next 2 chs, dc in next sc, yo, draw through all 4 lps on hook.

Beg dc3tog: Ch 3; holding back on hook last lp of each st, dc in each of next 2 chs, yo, draw through all 3 lps on hook.

Dc5tog: Holding back on hook last lp of each st, dc in each of next 2 chs, dc in next sc, dc in each of next 2 chs, yo, draw through all 6 lps on hook.

Skill Level

Intermediate

Size

Approximately 49" x 60" excluding fringe

Materials

- Spinrite Bernat Illusions bulky weight yarn (5 oz per skein): 7 skeins each deep mulberry #607 (A) and linen #600 (B)
- Size N/15 crochet hook or size needed to obtain gauge

Gauge

Shell = 2³⁄₄" with 2 strands held tog

Check gauge to save time.

Afghan

Row 1: Ch 133 (foundation ch), ch 3 more (turning ch-3), 2 dc in 4th ch from hook, sk 2 chs, sc in next ch, [sk 2 chs, shell in next ch, sk 2 chs, sc in next ch] rep across to last 3 chs, sk 2 chs, half shell in last ch, ch 1, turn. (21 shells, 1 half shell at each edge)

Row 2: Sc in first dc, [ch 5, sc in center dc of next shell] rep across to last shell, ch 5, sc in 3rd ch of turning ch-3, turn. (22 ch-5 sps)

Row 3: Beg dc3tog, *ch 2, sc in next ch, ch 2 **, dc5tog, rep from * across, ending last rep at **, dc3tog, turn. (21 dc5togs, 1 dc3tog at each edge)

Row 4: Beg half shell in top of first dc3tog, sc in next sc, [shell in top of next dc5tog, sc in next sc] rep across to last sc, half shell in top of beg dc3tog, ch 1, turn. (21 shells, 1 half shell at each edge)

Rep Rows 2–4 alternately until afghan measures approximately 49" or desired width, ending with a Row 3; fasten off.

Finishing
Fringe

Cut 10 (95") lengths of A. Holding all 10 strands tog, weave through first row of ch-5 sps, leaving an equal length at each end of afghan for fringe. Alternating A and B, rep for each row of ch-5 sps across. Tie each group of 10 strands in an overhand knot at each end. Tack knot to afghan. Trim fringe to desired length. ❖

Scrap Favorites

*T*urn those dozens of skeins of
scrap yarn odds and ends into
gorgeous afghans to warm your
family and friends!

Chapter 4

Indian Paintbrush

Design by Alma Shields

From the deserts of the southwest comes the inspiration for this Native-American-style afghan.

Pattern Notes

Afghan is worked from side to side, holding 3 strands tog throughout.

To change color in dc, work last dc before color change until last 2 lps before final yo rem on hook, drop working color to WS, yo with next color, complete dc.

When working from chart, color not in use may be carried loosely across back of work for not more than 3 sts, working over it with color in use until it is needed again. For larger sections, wind separate 3-strand balls of thread or use bobbins.

When beg rows of new colors and fastening off at ends of rows, leave 6" lengths for fringe.

When working from chart, read all odd-numbered (RS) rows from right to left, all even-numbered (WS) rows from left to right.

Afghan

Row 1 (RS): With B, ch 77, dc in 4th ch from hook, dc in each rem ch across, fasten off, turn. (75 dc, counting last 3 chs of foundation ch as first dc)

Skill Level

Intermediate

Size

48" x 59" excluding fringe

Materials

- Coats & Clark Red Heart Super Saver worsted weight yarn (8 oz per skein): 2 skeins each soft white #316 (A), windsor blue #380 (B), country blue #382 (C), and 1 skein each spruce #362 (D), rose pink #372 (E), country rose #374 (F), and buff #334 (G)
- Size Q crochet hook or size needed to obtain gauge

Gauge

5 dc = 4" with 3 strands held tog

Check gauge to save time.

Row 2: With WS facing, attach C with a sl st in first st, ch 3 (counts as first dc throughout), dc in each rem st across, turn. (75 dc)

Row 3: Ch 3, dc in each rem st across, fasten off, turn. (75 dc)

Row 4: With WS facing, attach E with a sl st in first st, ch 1, beg in same st, sc in each st across, fasten off, turn. (75 sc)

Row 5: With RS facing, rep Row 2.

Row 6: Rep Row 3.

Row 7: With RS facing, attach D with a sl st in first st, ch 3, dc in next st, changing to A, [dc in next st, changing to D; dc in each of next 3 sts, changing to A in 3rd st] rep across to last st, dc

Continued on page 76

Country Blend

Design by Maggie Weldon

Soft shades of green, blue and burgundy come together to create this lovely country afghan.

Pattern Notes

Join rnds with a sl st unless otherwise stated.

Afghan is worked with 2 strands held tog throughout.

Pattern Stitch

Shell: [{Dc, ch 1} 4 times, dc] in indicated st or sp.

Afghan

Row 1 (RS): With A, ch 98, sc in 2nd ch from hook, [sk 2 chs, shell in next ch, sk 2 chs, sc in next ch] rep across, fasten off, turn. (16 shells)

Row 2: With WS facing, attach MC with a sl st in first sc, ch 4 (counts as first dc, ch-1 throughout), *sk next ch-1 sp, sc in next ch-1 sp, ch 1, sc in next ch-1 sp, ch 1, dc in next sc **, ch 1, rep from * across, ending last rep at **, fasten off, turn.

Row 3: With RS facing, attach B with a sl st in first dc, ch 1, sc in same st, *sk

Skill Level

Beginner

Size

Approximately 46" x 62"

Materials

- Spinrite's Bernat Berella "4" worsted weight yarn (3.5 oz per skein): 5 skeins winter white #8941 (MC), and 4 skeins each deep sea green #8876 (A), navy #8965 (B), and burgundy #8927 (C)
- Size P crochet hook or size needed to obtain gauge

Gauge

Shell = 2¾" with 2 strands held tog

Check gauge to save time.

next ch-1 sp, shell in next ch-1 sp **, sc in next dc, rep from * across, ending last rep at **, sc in 3rd ch of turning ch-4, fasten off, turn. (16 shells)

Row 4: Rep Row 2.

Row 5: With C, rep Row 3.

Row 6: Rep Row 2.

Row 7: With A, rep Row 3.

Row 8: Rep Row 2.

Rows 9–78: Rep Rows 3–8 alternately, ending with a Row 6.

Border

Rnd 1: With RS facing attach C with a sl st in corner st at upper right corner, ch 3, [dc, ch 2, 2 dc] in same st, dc in each st and in each sp across to next corner, *[2 dc, ch 2, 2 dc] in corner st; *working over end sts of rows across, dc evenly sp across to next corner *, [2 dc, ch 2, 2 dc] in first rem lp of foundation ch, dc in each rem rem lp across to next corner, rep from * to *, join in 3rd ch of beg ch-3, fasten off. ❖

Granny's Scrap Afghan

Design by Maggie Weldon

Use up oodles of scrap yarn with this very easy-to-crochet granny square afghan!

Pattern Notes

Afghan is worked holding 3 strands tog throughout.

Join rnds with a sl st unless otherwise stated.

Square A (make 14)

Rnd 1 (RS): With light pink, ch 3, join to form a ring, ch 2 (counts as first hdc throughout), 2 hdc in ring, ch 1, [3 hdc in ring, ch 1] 3 times, join in 2nd ch of beg ch-2, fasten off. (12 hdc)

Rnd 2: With RS facing, attach pink with a sl st in any ch-1 sp, ch 2, [2 hdc, ch 1, 3 hdc] in same sp, [3 hdc, ch 1, 3 hdc] in each rem ch-1 sp around, join in 2nd ch of beg ch-2, fasten off. (24 hdc)

Rnd 3: With RS facing, attach white with a sl st in any ch-1 sp, ch 4 (counts as first tr throughout), [hdc, ch 2, hdc, tr] in same sp, *hdc in next st, tr in next st, hdc in next st, tr between same st and next st, hdc in next st, tr in next st, hdc in next st **, [tr, hdc, ch 2, hdc, tr] in next sp, rep from * around, ending last rep at **, join in 4th ch of beg ch-4, fasten off.

Square B (make 14)

Rnd 1: With light blue, rep Rnd 1 of square A.

Skill Level

Beginner

Size

Approximately 44" x 64" including border

Materials

- Worsted weight yarn: 13 (3.5 oz) skeins white, small amounts each light pink, pink, light green, green, light yellow, yellow, light blue, and blue
- Size Q crochet hook or size needed to obtain gauge
- Tapestry needle

Gauge

Square = 7" square with 3 strands held tog

Check gauge to save time.

Rnd 2: With blue, rep Rnd 2 of square A.

Rnd 3: Rep Rnd 3 of square A.

Square C (make 13)

Rnd 1: With light yellow, rep Rnd 1 of square A.

Rnd 2: With yellow, rep Rnd 2 of square A.

Rnd 3: Rep Rnd 3 of square A.

Square D (make 13)

Rnd 1: With light green, rep Rnd 1 of square A.

Assembly Diagram

B	A	D	C	B	A
C	D	A	B	C	D
B	A	D	C	B	A
C	D	A	B	C	D
B	A	D	C	B	A
C	D	A	B	C	D
B	A	D	C	B	A
C	D	A	B	C	D
B	A	D	C	B	A

Rnd 2: With green, rep Rnd 2 of square A.

Rnd 3: Rep Rnd 3 of square A.

Assembly

Using joining diagram as a guide, sew squares tog on WS with tapestry needle and white in 9 rows of 6 squares each.

Border

With RS facing, attach white with a sl st in any corner sp, ch 2, 2 hdc in same sp, hdc in each st and sp around, working 3 hdc in each corner, join in 2nd ch of beg ch-2, fasten off. ❖

Cluster Stitch Afghan

Design by Maggie Weldon

Pick a background color to match your decor, and then fill it in with a rainbow of scrap colors!

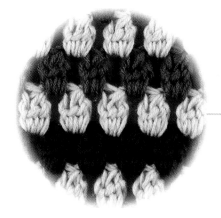

Skill Level

Intermediate

Size

Approximately 47" x 69"

Materials

- Worsted weight yarn (3.5 oz per skein): 9 skeins beige (MC) and 2 skeins each 8 different CCs
- Size P/16 crochet hook or size needed to obtain gauge

Gauge

4 cls = 4½" with 2 strands held tog

Check gauge to save time.

Pattern Notes

Join rnds with a sl st unless otherwise stated.

Afghan is worked with 2 strands held tog throughout.

Pattern Stitch

Cl: Holding back on hook last lp of each st, 3 dc in indicated st or sp, yo, draw through all 4 lps on hook.

Afghan

Row 1 (RS): With MC, ch 81 (foundation ch), ch 3 more (turning ch), cl in 4th ch from hook, [ch 1, sk next ch, cl in next ch] rep across to last 2 chs, ch 1, sk next ch, dc in last ch, fasten off MC. (40 cls, 1 dc at each edge, counting turning ch-3 as first dc)

Row 2: With RS facing, attach any CC with a sl st in 3rd ch of turning ch-3, ch 4 (counts as first dc, ch-1 throughout), [cl in next ch-1 sp, ch 1] rep across to last ch-1 sp, cl in last ch-1 sp, dc in last dc, fasten off. (40 cls, 1 dc at each edge)

Row 3: With RS facing, attach MC with a sl st in 3rd ch of turning ch-4, ch 3 (counts as first dc throughout), [cl in next ch-1 sp, ch 1] rep across, dc in last dc, fasten off MC. (40 cls, 1 dc at each edge)

Row 4: With RS facing, attach next CC with a sl st in 3rd ch of turning ch-3, ch 4, [cl in next ch-1 sp, ch 1] rep across to last sp, cl in last sp, dc in last dc, fasten off. (40 cls, 1 dc at each edge)

Rep Rows 3 and 4 alternately until afghan measures approximately 67" or desired length, ending with a Row 3.

Border

Rnd 1: With RS facing, attach MC with a sl st in first st of last row, ch 1, 3 sc in same st, sc in each st and sp across to next corner, *3 sc in corner st, sc evenly sp over row ends to next corner *, 3 sc in corner st, sc in each rem lp across foundation ch to next corner, rep from * to *, join in beg sc.

Rnd 2: Ch 1; beg in same st as joining, work 1 rnd rev sc, join in beg rev sc, fasten off. ❖

Jewelled Waves

Design by Charlene G. Finiello

Capture the essence of sunlight dancing off the ocean waves with this enchanting afghan!

Pattern Note

Afghan is worked from side to side holding 2 strands tog throughout.

Afghan

Row 1: With 2 strands MC held tog, ch 100, sc in 2nd ch from hook, sc in next ch, *hdc in each of next 2 chs, dc in each of next 2 chs, tr in each of next 3 chs, dc in each of next 2 chs, hdc in each of next 2 chs **, sc in each of next 3 chs, rep from * across to last 2 chs, ending last rep at **, sc in each of last 2 chs, cut 1 strand MC, turn. (99 sts)

Row 2: With rem strand MC and 1 strand B held tog, ch 4 (counts as first tr throughout), tr in next st, *dc in each of next 2 sts, hdc in each of next 2 sts, sc in each of next 3 sts, hdc in each of next 2 sts, dc in each of next 2 sts **, tr in each of next 3 sts, rep from * across to last 2 sts, ending last rep at **, tr in each of last 2 sts, cut B, turn. (99 sts)

Row 3: With 2 strands MC held tog, ch 1, sc in each of first 2 sts, *hdc in each of next 2 sts, dc in each of next 2 sts, tr in each of next 3 sts, dc in each of next 2 sts, hdc in each of next 2 sts **, sc in each of next 3 sts, rep from * across to last 2 sts, ending last rep at **, sc in each of last 2 sts, cut 1 strand MC, turn. (99 sts)

Row 4: With rem strand MC and 1

Skill Level

Beginner

Size

Approximately 43" x 55" excluding fringe

Materials

- Coats & Clark Red Heart Super Saver worsted weight yarn (8 oz per skein): 4 skeins black #312 (MC), and 1 skein each royal blue #385 (A), teal #388 (B), and burgundy #376 (C)
- Size P/16 crochet hook or size needed to obtain gauge

Gauge

9 sts = 5" in pattern st with 2 strands held tog

Check gauge to save time.

strand C held tog, rep Row 2, cut C, turn. (99 sts)

Row 5: Rep Row 3.

Row 6: With rem strand MC and 1 strand A held tog, rep Row 2, cut A, turn. (99 sts)

Row 7: Rep Row 3.

Rows 8 & 9: Rep Rows 2 and 3.

Rows 10–51: Rep Rows 4–9 alternately 7 times; fasten off at end of Row 51.

Finishing
Fringe

Cut 10 (14") lengths of MC. Holding all 10 lengths tog, fold strands in half. Beg over end tr or beg ch-4 of Row 2 on either short edge of afghan, insert hook from WS to RS over end st, draw folded end of strands through st to form a lp, pull free ends through lp and tighten. Rep for every other row across edge. Rep across opposite short edge. ❖

Jiffy Scrap Shells

Design by Tammy Hildebrand

Cuddle up in this oh-so-soft afghan made from remnants of acrylic, mohair-like yarn!

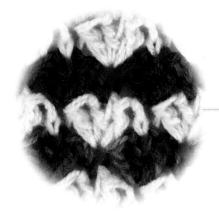

Skill Level
Beginner

Size
Approximately 42" x 65" excluding fringe

Materials
- Lion Brand Jiffy mohair look yarn (3 oz per skein): 10 skeins fisherman #99 (MC) and 32 oz assorted CCs
- Size Q crochet hook or size needed to obtain gauge

Gauge
Shell = $2\frac{1}{4}$" with 2 strands held tog

Check gauge to save time

Pattern Note
Afghan is worked with 2 strands held tog throughout.

Pattern Stitches
Shell: 3 dc in indicated st or sp.

Half shell: 2 dc in indicated st or sp.

Beg half shell: [Ch 3 (counts as first dc), dc] in indicated st or sp.

Afghan
Row 1 (RS): With MC, ch 53 (foundation ch), ch 3 more (turning ch-3), dc in 4th ch from hook, sk next ch, sc in next ch, [sk next ch, shell in next ch, sk next ch, sc in next ch] rep across to last 2 chs, sk next ch, half shell in last ch, fasten off MC, turn. (12 shells, 1 half shell at each edge)

Row 2: With RS facing, attach any CC with a sl st in 3rd ch of turning ch-3, ch 1, sc in same st, shell in next sc, [sc in center dc of next shell, shell in next sc] rep across to last sc, sc in last dc of half shell, fasten off. (13 shells)

Row 3: With RS facing, attach MC with a sl st in first sc, beg half shell in same st, sc in center dc of next shell, [shell in next sc, sc in center dc of next shell] rep across to last shell, half shell in last sc, fasten off. (12 shells, 1 half shell at each edge)

Rep Rows 2 and 3 until afghan measures approximately 65" or desired length, ending with a Row 2.

Last Row: With RS facing, attach MC with a sl st in first sc, ch 3, sc in each dc and dc in each sc across, fasten off.

Finishing
Fringe
Cut 4 (18") lengths of any CC. Holding all 4 strands tog, fold strands in half. Insert hook from WS to RS in first st across either short edge, draw folded end through st on hook to form lp, draw free ends of strands through lp, pull tightly to close. Alternating CCs, rep for each st across edge. Rep across opposite short edge. ❖

CHAPTER 4

Rainbow Lightning

Design by Alma Shields

Turn your basketful of scrap yarn into this eye-catching afghan! Kids especially love it!

Pattern Notes

Join rnds with a sl st unless otherwise stated.

Afghan is worked holding 3 strands tog throughout.

When working from chart, read all odd-numbered (RS) rows from right to left, all even-numbered (WS) rows from left to right.

Carry MC loosely across back of work when not in use, working over it with CC in use until it is needed again. Do not carry CCs not in use across back of work; wind 3-strand ball of yarn for each separate CC section.

To change color in ch-2, ch 1 with working color, drop working color to WS, yo with next color, draw through lp on hook.

To change color in hdc, work last st before color change with working color until last 3 lps before final yo rem on hook, drop working color to WS, yo with next color, draw through all 3 lps on hook.

Afghan

Row 1 (RS): With MC, ch 60, hdc in 3rd ch from hook, changing to C, [hdc

Skill Level

Intermediate

Size

Approximately 46" x 60"

Materials

• Coats & Clark Red Heart Super Saver worsted weight yarn (8 oz per skein): 6 skeins black #312 (MC), 1 skein each cherry red #319 (A), vibrant orange #354 (B), bright yellow #324 (C), spring green #367 (D), and royal blue #385 (E)

• Size Q crochet hook or size needed to obtain gauge

Gauge

7 hdc = 5" with 3 strands held tog
Check gauge to save time.

in next ch with C, hdc in next ch with MC] 4 times, hdc in each of next 3 chs with MC, changing to B in last st, [hdc in next st with B, hdc in next st with MC] 4 times, hdc in each of next 3 chs with MC, changing to A in last st, [hdc in next ch with A, hdc in next ch with MC] 4 times, hdc in each of next 3 chs with MC, changing to E in last st, [hdc in next ch with E, hdc in next ch with MC] 4 times, hdc in each of next 3 chs with MC, changing to D in last st, [hdc

in next st with D, hdc in next st with MC] 4 times, hdc in each of next 3 chs with MC, changing to 2nd ball of C in last st, hdc in next ch with C, hdc in last ch with MC, turn. (59 hdc, counting last 2 chs of foundation ch as first hdc)

Row 2: Ch 2, changing to C (counts as first hdc throughout), continue across row working from chart (page 77), changing colors as indicated, turn. (59 hdc)

Rows 3–60: Work from chart, changing colors as indicated; at end of Row 60, fasten off CCs; do not fasten off MC; ch 1, turn.

Border

Rnd 1 (RS): 2 sc in first st, sc in each st across to next corner, 3 sc in corner st; *working over end st of each row across, sc evenly sp across to next corner *, 3 sc in first rem lp of foundation ch, sc in each rem lp of foundation ch across to last st, 3 sc in last st, rep from * to *, sc in same st as beg sc, join in beg sc, turn.

Rnd 2: Ch 2, hdc in same st as joining, *hdc in each st across to next corner **, 3 hdc in corner st, rep from * around, ending last rep at **, hdc in same st as beg ch-2, join in 2nd ch of beg ch-2, turn.

Rnd 3: Rep Rnd 2, do not turn.

Rnd 4: With RS facing, sl st in each st around, join in beg sl st, fasten off. ❖

Chart A on page 77

Indian Paintbrush

Continued from page 62

in last st with A, fasten off D, ch 1 with A, turn. (75 dc)

Row 8: Sc in each st across, fasten off, turn. (75 sc)

Row 9: With RS facing, attach B with a sl st in first st, ch 3, dc in each rem st across, fasten off, turn. (75 dc)

Row 10: With WS facing and F, rep Row 9.

Row 11: With E, rep Row 9.

Row 12: With WS facing and G, rep Row 9.

Row 13: Rep Row 9.

Row 14: With WS facing, attach A with a sl st in first st, ch 1, beg in same st, sc in each st across, fasten off, turn.

Row 15: Rep Row 7; fasten off A and D, turn.

Row 16: With WS facing and C, rep Row 9.

Rows 17–25: Work from chart, changing colors as indicated.

Row 26: Rep Row 16.

Rows 27 & 28: Rep Rows 7 and 8.

Rows 29–33: Working in reverse order and beg with Row 13, rep Rows 13–9.

Rows 34 & 35: Rep Rows 14 and 15.

Rows 36–40: Rep Rows 2–6.

Row 41: Rep Row 9.

Finishing
Fringe

Matching color of fringe to color of row being worked, cut 8 (12") lengths of yarn for first row of either short edge. Holding all lengths tog, fold in half, insert hook from WS to RS through end st of row, draw folded end of strands through st to form lp, draw free ends through lp and pull to tighten. Rep for each row across both short edges of afghan. ❖

```
COLOR & STITCH KEY
☐ Dc with A
◉ Dc with D
⊠ Dc with F
⊡ Dc with G
◎ Dc with B
```

Chart A

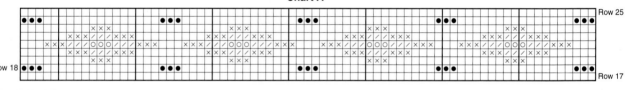

Embellish a Plain Afghan

To jazz up a plain afghan, crochet or embroider flowers, bows or other adornments and stitch randomly over the afghan. You can use up scraps of novelty yarns and those twisted with metallic filament; however, be sure the care properties are the same (machine washable and dryable).

Embroidered flower: Thread tapestry needle with 2–3 strands of yarn. Working with these strands doubled, embroider French knots where desired, wrapping yarn once around needle. For leaves, use doubled green yarn to embroider a straight stitch for each leaf.

Rosebud: Make a 5"–6" chain. Dc in 4th ch from hook, dc in each ch across (experiment with length of chain and the number of sts until desired flower size is achieved; extra chains can be cut off if not needed). Fasten off, leaving 6" length. With tapestry needle, weave end through sts of last row and pull tightly to gather. Roll up into a spiral resembling a rosebud. Tack at center to secure. Sew or tie securely to afghan.

Chain bow: Using one or more strands of yarn in desired colors, make a chain (experiment with length depending on how long you want bow). Tie into bow and sew or tie securely to afghan.

Small bow: Ch 9 (experiment with one or two strands and number of chains depending on width of bow you want). Dc in 4th ch from hook. For large bow, work 5 rows (or number of rows desired, depending on weight of yarn). Fasten off. Finishing:

Tightly wrap another strand of yarn a few times around center of bow. Sew or tie to afghan.

Two-tone flower: Outer circle: Make a chain 6" long (or experiment with length). Dc in 4th ch from hook, dc in each ch across. Fasten off, leaving an 8" length. With tapestry needle, weave end through sts of last row and pull tightly to gather into a circle. Tack first and last sts together.

Inner circle: Using CC, crochet 3" chain (or half as long as chain made for outer circle). Work 1 row of sc; fasten off, leaving an end. Weave end through sts of last row and pull to gather into a circle. Tack first and last sts tog. Tack inner circle to center of outer circle and attach to afghan.

— Isabelle Wolters

Rainbow Lightning

Continued from page 74

COLOR KEY
- ■ Red
- ▨ Orange
- ☐ Yellow
- ▨ Green
- ■ Blue
- ☐ Black

Chart A

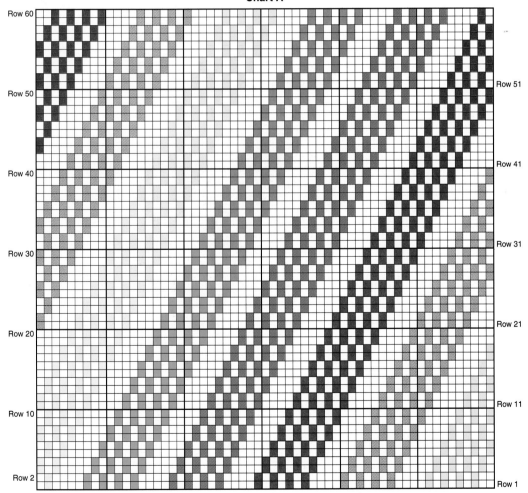

Baby Brights

*W*hether you lovingly crochet a coverlet for your own precious little one, or as a gift for a mother-to-be, there are few gifts as special as a hand-crocheted baby afghan.

Spring Bouquet

Design by Josie Rabier

Delicate motifs come together in this delightful baby blanket you'll love to wrap Baby in!

Pattern Note

Join rnds with a sl st unless otherwise stated.

Pattern Stitches

Tr cl: Holding back on hook last lp of each st, 3 tr in next st, yo, draw through all 4 lps on hook.

Split pc: Holding back on hook last lp of each st, 3 dc in each of next 2 ch-1 sps, remove hook from lp, insert hook from RS to WS in top of first of last 6 dc made, pick up dropped lp, draw through st on hook.

Beg split pc: Ch 3; holding back on hook last lp of each st, 2 dc in same sp as ch-3, 3 dc in next ch-1 sp, remove hook from lp, insert hook from RS to WS in 3rd ch of ch-3, pick up dropped lp, draw through st on hook.

Flower (make 5 A, 12 B, and 4 each C and D)

Rnd 1 (RS): Ch 6, join to form a ring, ch 3 (counts as first dc), 23 dc in ring, join in 3rd ch of beg ch-3. (24 dc)

Rnd 2: *Ch 5, tr cl in next st, ch 5 **, sl st in front lp only of each of next 2 sts, rep from * around, ending last rep

Skill Level

Intermediate

Size

Aproximately 40" square including border

Materials

- Lion Brand Jamie 4-ply worsted weight yarn (6 oz per skein): 3 skeins antique white #099 (MC), 1 skein each pastel green #169 (A), pastel yellow #157 (B), pastel blue #106 (C), and pastel pink #101 (D)
- Size K/10½ crochet hook or size needed to obtain gauge
- Sewing needle and white sewing thread

Gauge

Flower = 5" in diameter

Check gauge to save time.

at **, sl st in front lp only of next st, join in same st as joining st of Rnd 1, fasten off. (8 petals)

First Square

Rnd 1: With RS facing, working behind petals, attach MC with a sl st in rem lp of 2nd dc on Rnd 1 of any flower D between any 2 Rnd 2 petals, ch 5, [sl st in rem lp of each of next 2 dc of Rnd 1 between next 2 Rnd 2 petals, ch 5] rep around, ending with ch 5, sl st in rem lp of next dc of Rnd 1 between next 2 Rnd 2 petals, join in same st as beg sl st. (8 ch-5 sps)

Continued on page 96

Loving Kisses

Design by Connie L. Folse

Stitch by stitch, this pretty afghan is a warm and snuggly expression of your love for Baby!

Pattern Notes

Afghan is worked with 2 strands held tog throughout.

Join rnds with a sl st unless otherwise stated.

Pattern Stitches

Treble tr (trtr): Yo 4 times, insert hook in indicated st, yo, draw up a lp, [yo, draw through 2 lps on hook] 5 times.

X-st: Trtr in 4th sk dc of next 4-dc group on row before last, ch 2, trtr in first sk dc of same 4-dc group on row before last.

Afghan

Row 1 (RS): Ch 100 (foundation ch), ch 3 more (turning ch-3), dc in 4th ch from hook, dc in each rem ch across, turn. (101 dc, counting turning ch-3 as first dc)

Row 2: Ch 3 (counts as first dc throughout), dc in each of next 2 dc, ch 4, sk next 4 dc, [dc in each of next 3 dc, ch 4, sk next 4 dc] rep across to last 3 sts, dc in each of next 2 dc, dc in 3rd ch of turning ch-3, turn.

Row 3: Ch 3, dc in each of next 2 dc, X-st, [dc in each of next 3 dc, X-st] rep across to last 3 sts, dc in each of next 2 dc, dc in 3rd ch of turning ch-3, turn. (14 X-sts)

Row 4: Ch 3, dc in each st and in each ch across, turn. (101 dc)

Row 5: Ch 3, dc in each dc across, turn. (101 dc)

Rows 6 & 7: Rep Rows 2 and 3.

Rows 8–56: Rep Rows 4–7 alternately, ending with a Row 4; do not fasten off at end of Row 56; ch 1, turn.

Border

Rnd 1: Sc in each dc across to last dc; *working over row ends, work 114 sc evenly sp across to next corner *, sc in first rem lp of foundation ch, sc in each rem lp of foundation ch across to last st, rep from * to *, join in beg sc.

Rnd 2: Ch 3, 2 dc in same st as joining, *[sc in next st, 2 dc in next st, sc in next st] 33 times, 3 dc in next st, [sc in next st, 2 dc in next st, sc in next st] 38 times **, 3 dc in next st, rep from * around, ending last rep at **, join in 3rd ch of beg ch-3, fasten off. ❖

Skill Level

Intermediate

Size

38½" x 44" including border

Materials

- Coats & Clark Red Heart Baby Sport sport weight yarn (1.75 oz per skein): 18 skeins baby yellow #224
- Size H/8 crochet hook or size needed to obtain gauge

Gauge

11 dc = 4" with 2 strands held tog
Check gauge to save time.

Waiting Line Afghan

Here's a tip for all those wannabe crocheters who say they are too busy: I have crocheted the squares for an entire afghan just while waiting in lines! Instead of a purse, I carry a large bag—fabric works best—with two large zipper pouches inside. In one pouch I carry my usual purse items (wallet, keys, change purse, etc.), and in the other, a 3" x 5" card with the pattern, a crochet hook and a small scissors. I carry the yarn itself in the main compartment of the bag, which is large enough to allow plenty of room for the yarn.

I carry this everywhere I go; it's lightweight and convenient. The 15 minutes spent waiting in the checkout line with a grocery cart are perfect for adding a few rows. Government and doctors' offices are notorious for long waits, and great for completing a whole square. And if you participate in a carpool, you can add more rows on those days when you ride instead of drive!

Keep finished squares and extra yarn at home. This keeps your work bag light and manageable. When all the squares are completed, just attach them and your "Waiting Line Afghan" is finished!

—Carli A. Damien

Cloud Nine

Design by Laura Gebhardt

A frilly ruffle makes this darling shell-stitch blanket unique and extra-special!

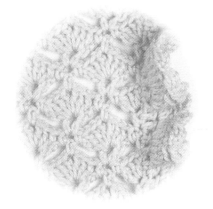

Skill Level
Intermediate

Size
33" x 40" including border

Materials
- Worsted weight yarn: 25 oz. pink
- Size G/6 crochet hook or size needed to obtain gauge

Gauge
Shell = 1$\frac{3}{8}$"

Check gauge to save time.

Pattern Note
Join rnds with a sl st unless otherwise stated.

Pattern Stitches
Shell: [3 dc, ch 1, 3 dc] in indicated st or sp.

V-st: [Hdc, ch 1, hdc] in indicated sp or st.

Afghan
Row 1 (RS): Ch 152, sc in 2nd ch from hook, sc in next ch, *sk 3 chs, shell in next ch, sk 3 chs, sc in next ch **, ch 1, sk next ch, sc in next ch, rep from * across, ending last rep at **, sc in last ch, turn. (15 shells)

Row 2: Ch 2 (counts as first hdc throughout), hdc in first sc, *ch 3, sc in shell sp, ch 3 **, V-st in next ch-1 sp, rep from * across, ending last rep at **, 2 hdc in last sc, turn.

Row 3: Ch 3 (counts as first dc throughout), 3 dc in first st, *sc in next ch-3 sp, ch 1, sc in next ch-3 sp **, shell in next V-st sp, rep from * across, ending last rep at **, 4 dc in 2nd ch of turning ch-2, ch 1, turn. (14 shells)

Row 4: Sc in first dc, *ch 3, V-st in next ch-1 sp, ch 3 **, sc in next shell sp, rep from * across, ending last rep at **, sc in 3rd ch of turning ch-3, ch 1, turn.

Row 5: Sc in first st, *sc in next ch-3 sp, shell in next V-st sp, sc in next ch-3 sp **, ch 1, rep from * across, ending last rep at **, sc in last sc, turn. (15 shells)

Rows 6–103: Rep Rows 2–5 alternately, ending with a Row 3; do not fasten off at end of Row 103; do not turn.

Border
Rnd 1: Ch 3, *dc evenly sp over row end sts across to next corner, 3 dc in corner st *, working in rem lps of foundation ch, dc in each st across to next corner, 3 dc in corner st, rep from * to *, dc in each st and ch-1 sp across last row, 2 dc in same st as beg ch-3, join in 3rd ch of beg ch-3.

Rnd 2: Ch 3, 2 dc in same st as joining, 3 dc in each rem dc around, join in 3rd ch of beg ch-3.

Rnd 3: Ch 1, [sc, ch 3, dc] in same st as joining, [sk 2 sts, {sc, ch 3, dc} in next st] rep around, join in beg sc, fasten off. ❖

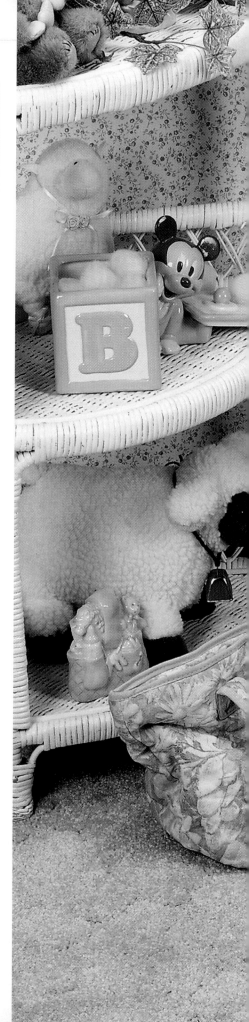

Sweet Dreams

Design by Vicki Blizzard

Tuck Baby in at night or nap time under this snuggly-soft granny square afghan!

Pattern Notes

Join rnds with a sl st unless otherwise stated.

To change color in sc, work last st before color change as follows: insert hook in indicated st or sp, yo with working color, draw up a lp, drop working color to WS, yo with next color, complete sc.

Pattern Stitch

Shell: 5 dc in indicated st or sp.

Large Block (make 2 of each color combination)

Rnd 1 (RS): With A (B, C, D), ch 4, join to form a ring, ch 3 (counts as first dc), [3 dc, ch 2, {4 dc, ch 2} 3 times] in ring, join in 3rd ch of beg ch-3, fasten off.

Rnd 2: With RS facing, attach MC with a sl st in any corner ch-2 sp, ch 1, beg in same sp, *[2 sc, ch 2, 2 sc] in corner sp, sc in back lp only of each dc across to next ch-2 sp, rep from * around, join in beg sc, fasten off.

Rnd 3: With RS facing, attach A (B, C, D) with a sl st in any corner ch-2 sp, ch 5 (counts as first dc, ch-2), dc in same sp, *dc in back lp only of each sc across to next ch-2 sp **, [dc, ch 2, dc] in ch-2 sp, rep from * around, ending last rep at **, join in 3rd ch of beg ch-5, fasten off.

Rnd 4: Rep Rnd 2.

Small Block A (make 4 of each color combination)

Skill Level

Intermediate

Size

Approximately 36" square including border

Materials

- Patons Melody yarn (3½ oz/85 yds per skein): 5 skeins white #901 (MC) and 1 skein each lavendar #907 (A), pink #905 (B), mint #906 (C) and blue #904 (D)
- Size N/15 crochet hook or size needed to give gauge
- Tapestry needle

Gauge

Rnd 1 of large block = 3" square
Check gauge to save time.

Rnds 1 & 2: Rep Rnds 1 and 2 of large block.

Small Block B (make 4 of each color combination)

Rnd 1: With MC, rep Rnd 1 of large block

Rnd 2: With A (B, C, D), rep Rnd 2 of large block.

Assembly

With tapestry needle and MC, using joining diagram as a guide, whipstitch blocks tog through back lps.

Border

Rnd 1: With RS facing, attach MC with a sl st in any corner ch-2 sp, ch 3, [dc, ch 2, 2 dc] in same sp, *dc in back lp only of each st across to next corner sp **, [2 dc, ch 2, 2 dc] in corner sp, rep from * around, ending last rep at **, join in 3rd ch of beg ch-3, fasten off.

Rnd 2: With RS facing, attach A with a sl st in back lp only of st on Rnd 1 of border at point where blue and mint sections of afghan meet (see joining diagram), ch 1; working in back lps only around, *sc in each st across to corner sp, 5 sc in corner sp, sc in each st across to next point on afghan where 2 different color sections meet, changing to next color indicated on joining diagram, rep from * around, join in beg sc, fasten off.

Rnd 3: With RS facing, attach MC with a sl st in any sc, ch 1, sc in same st, *sk 2 sts, shell in next st, sk 2 sts, sc in next st, rep from * around, adjusting number of sts sk at end of rnd, if necessary to end with a shell; join in beg sc, fasten off. ❖

Continued on page 97

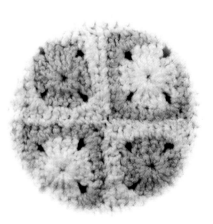

Blue Skies

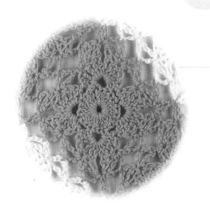

Design by Josie Rabier

Take this sweet blanket along as you treat Baby to an afternoon in the sunshine!

Pattern Note

Join rnds with a sl st unless otherwise stated.

Pattern Stitches

Shell: [Dc, 4 tr, ch 3, 4 tr, dc] in indicated sp.

Beg shell: [Ch 3, 4 tr, ch 3, 4 tr, dc] in indicated sp.

Center Diagonal Row
First Block

Rnd 1 (RS): With A, ch 4, join to form a ring, ch 3 (counts as first dc), 23 dc in ring, join in 3rd ch of beg ch-3. (24 dc)

Rnd 2: Ch 3, [sk 2 dc, sl st in next dc, ch 3] rep around, join in same st as joining st of Rnd 1. (8 ch-3 sps)

Rnd 3: Sl st in first ch-3 sp, beg shell in same sp, sl st in next sp, [shell in next sp, sl st in next sp] rep around, join in 3rd ch of beg ch-3. (4 shells)

Rnd 4: Sl st in each of first 2 tr, ch 5, tr in same st as last sl st, *[sl st, ch 5, sl st, ch 5, tr] in corner ch-3 sp, sk 2 tr, [sl st, ch 5, tr] in next tr **, [sl st, ch 5, tr] in 2nd tr of next shell, rep from * around, ending last rep at **, join in 2nd tr of next shell, fasten off.

2nd Block

Rnds 1–3: Rep Rnds 1–3 of first block.
Joining Rnd

Rnd 4: Sl st in each of first 2 tr, ch 5, tr in same st as last sl st, sl st in corner

Skill Level

Intermediate

Size

Approximately 39" square including border

Materials

- Lion Brand Jamie 4-ply worsted weight yarn (6 oz per skein): 2 skeins each antique white #099 (A) and pastel blue #106 (B)
- Size K/10½ crochet hook or size needed to obtain gauge

Gauge

Block = 5½" square
Check gauge to save time.

ch-3 sp, ch 2, sl st in center ch of corresponding ch-5 sp on previous block, ch 2, sl st in same corner ch-3 sp on working block, ch 2, sl st in center ch of corresponding ch-5 sp on previous block, ch 2, tr in same corner ch-3 sp on working block, sk 2 tr, sl st in next tr on working block, *ch 2, sl st in center ch of corresponding ch-5 sp on previous block, ch 2, tr in same tr on working block *, sl st in 2nd tr of next shell, rep from * to *, sl st in corner ch-3 sp on working block, ch 2, sl st in corresponding ch-5 sp on previous block, ch 2, [sl st, ch 5, tr] in same corner ch-3 sp on working block (1 side joined), continue around as for Rnd 4 of first block.

Rem 7 Blocks

Make and join 7 more blocks as for 2nd block.

Rem Diagonal Rows

Following joining diagram for color placement, make and join 32 more blocks (12 A, 20 B) as for 2nd block, joining on as many sides as are indicated on joining diagram.

Border

With RS facing, attach A with a sl st in center ch of corner ch-5 sp at point indicated on joining diagram, *ch 5, tr in same st, [{sl st, ch 5, tr} in center ch of next ch-5 sp] rep across to next joining st between motifs, sl st in joining st, ch 2, turn, sl st in 3rd ch of last ch-5 made, turn, ch 2, tr in same joining st between motifs, sl st in center ch of next ch-5 sp on next motif, rep from * around, join in st at base of beg ch-5, fasten off. ❖

Assembly Diagram

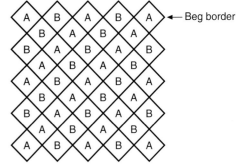

← Beg border

Lilac Lace

Design by Lori Zeller

Coordinate the colors of this cheerful afghan to Baby's nursery. Or, use up scrap pastels for a rainbow-colored blanket.

Pattern Note

Join rnds with a sl st unless otherwise stated.

Pattern Stitches

V-st: [Dc, ch 1, dc] in indicated st or sp.

Beg V-st: [Ch 4, dc] in indicated st or sp.

Double V-st: [{Dc, ch 1} 3 times, dc] in indicated st or sp.

First Panel

Rnd 1 (RS): With MC, ch 8 (foundation ch), ch 4 more (counts as first dc, ch-1), dc in 5th ch from hook, [ch 1, dc] twice in same ch, sk 3 chs, [dc, ch 1] 3 times in next ch, sk 2 chs, sl st in last ch, ch 1; working in rem lps across opposite side of foundation ch, sk 2 chs, [{dc, ch 1} twice, dc] in next ch, sk 3 chs, [dc, ch 1] 3 times in next ch, join in 3rd ch of beg ch-4 (1 link made).

Rnds 2–12: Rep Rnd 1 for a total of 12 links; do not fasten off at end of Rnd 12.

Rnd 13: Sl st in first ch-1 sp, ch 1, sc in same sp, [ch 3, sc in next ch-1 sp] 4 times, ch 3, *[sk next ch-1 sp on same

Skill Level

Intermediate

Size

32" x 40"

Materials

- Worsted weight yarn: 11 oz lilac (MC) and 6 oz white (CC)
- Size K/10½ crochet hook or size needed to obtain gauge

Gauge

Rnd 1 of first panel = 1½" x 3"

Check gauge to save time.

link and next ch-1 sp on next link, {sc in next ch-1 sp, ch 3} 4 times] 10 times, sk next ch-1 sp on same link and next ch-1 sp on next link *, [sc in next ch-1 sp, ch 3] 10 times, rep from * to *, [sc in next ch-1 sp, ch 3] 5 times, join in beg sc. (100 ch-3 sps)

Rnd 14: Sl st in first ch-3 sp, [beg V-st, ch 1, V-st] in same sp, *[V-st in next ch-3 sp] 47 times *, double V-st in each of next 3 sps, rep from * to *, double V-st in each of last 2 sps, join in 3rd ch of beg ch-4, fasten off.

Rnd 15: With RS facing, attach CC with a sl st in first ch-1 sp after joining, ch 1, sc in same sp, ch 2, [sc in next ch-1 sp, ch 2] rep around, join in beg sc, fasten off.

Rem 6 Panels

Rnds 1–15: Rep Rnds 1–15 of first panel; do not fasten off at end of Rnd 15.

Joining

Row 1: Sl st in each of next 2 chs, in next sc, and in next ch-2 sp, ch 1, sc in same sp as last sl st, ch 2, sc in corresponding sp on previous panel (6th ch-2 sp to the right of Rnd 15 joining st on previous panel), [ch 2, sc in next ch-2 sp on working panel, ch 2, sc in next ch-2 sp on previous panel] 49 times, fasten off; at end of last panel, do not fasten off.

Border

Rnd 1: Ch 2, sc in same ch-2 sp on working panel as last sc on working panel, ch 2, [sc in next ch-2 sp, ch 2] rep around, join in last sc of last joining row.

Rnd 2: Sl st in next ch-2 sp, ch 1, beg in same sp, [sc, ch 1, hdc] in each ch-2 sp around, join in beg sc, fasten off. ❖

CHAPTER 5

Rainbow Baby

Design by Kathleen Garen

Babies that are several months old will be fascinated by the bright color block in the center of this vibrant afghan!

Pattern Note

Join rnds with a sl st unless otherwise stated.

Pattern Stitches

Joined dc (jdc): Holding back on hook last lp of each st, dc in each of 2 indicated sps, yo, draw through all 3 lps on hook.

Beg jdc: Ch 2, dc in next sp.

Dc cl: Holding back on hook last lp of each st, 2 dc in indicated st or sp, yo, draw through all 3 lps on hook.

Beg dc cl: [Ch 2, dc] in indicated st or sp.

V-st: [Dc, ch 2, dc] in indicated sp.

Joined sc (jsc): Draw up a lp in each of 2 indicated sps, yo, draw through all 3 lps on hook.

Afghan

Rnd 1 (RS): With A, ch 5, join to form a ring, [beg dc cl, ch 1, dc cl, ch 2, {dc cl, ch 1, dc cl, ch 2} 3 times] in ring, join in top of beg dc cl, fasten off. (8 dc cls, 4 ch-1 sps, 4 corner ch-2 sps)

Rnd 2: With RS facing, attach B with a sl st in any ch-1 sp, beg jdc, *ch 1, [V-st, ch 1] in corner ch-2 sp, jdc over same sp as last dc and next ch-1 sp, ch 1 **, jdc over same ch-1 sp and next corner ch-2 sp, rep from * around, ending last rep at **, join in top of beg jdc, fasten off. (8 jdc, 4 V-sts)

Rnd 3: With RS facing, attach C with a sl st in first ch-1 sp to the right of any corner ch-2 sp, beg jdc, *ch 1, [V-st, ch

1] in corner ch-2 sp, jdc over same sp as last dc and next ch-1 sp, ch 1, [jdc over same sp as last half of last jdc and next ch-1 sp, ch 1] rep across to next corner ch-2 sp **, jdc over same sp as last half of last jdc and corner ch-2 sp, rep from * around, ending last rep at **, join in top of beg jdc, fasten off. (16 jdc, 4 V-sts)

Rnd 4: With D, rep Rnd 3. (24 jdc, 4 V-sts)

Rnd 5: With E, rep Rnd 3. (32 jdc, 4 V-sts)

Rnd 6: With F, rep Rnd 3. (40 jdc, 4 V-sts)

Rnd 7: With G, rep Rnd 3. (48 jdc, 4 V-sts)

Rnd 8: With MC, rep Rnd 3, do not fasten off. (56 jdc, 4 V-sts)

Skill Level

Intermediate

Size

Approximately 36" square

Materials

- Worsted weight mohair-like yarn (3 oz per skein): 5 skeins white (MC), 1 skein each red (A), red-orange (B), orange (C), yellow (D), green (E), blue (F), and lilac (G)
- Size J/10 crochet hook or size needed to obtain gauge

Gauge

Rnds 1–3 = 4¼" square

Check gauge to save time.

Rnds 9–20: Sl st in first ch-1 sp, beg jdc, rep Rnd 3 from * around, do not fasten off. (152 jdc, 4 V-sts at end of Rnd 20)

Rnd 21: Sl st in first ch-1 sp, beg jdc, rep Rnd 3 from * around, fasten off. (160 jdc, 4 V-sts)

Rnds 22–28: Rep Rnd 3 in the following color sequence: A, B, C, D, E, F, and G. (216 jdc, 4 V-sts at end of Rnd 28)

Rnds 29 & 30: Rep Rnds 8 and 9. (232 jdc, 4 V-sts at end of Rnd 30)

Border

Sl st in first ch-1 sp, jsc over same sp and corner ch-2 sp, *ch 3, sc in corner ch-2 sp, ch 3, jsc over corner ch-2 sp and next ch-1 sp, ch 3, [jsc over same ch-1 sp and next ch-1 sp, ch 3] rep across to next corner ch-2 sp **, jsc over same ch-1 sp as last half of last jsc and corner ch-2 sp, rep from * around, ending last rep at **, join in beg jsc, fasten off.

Ruffles
First Ruffle

With RS facing, attach MC with a sl st in any corner ch-2 sp on Rnd 7 to the right of first dc of V-st, ch 1, sc in same sp, *ch 3, sc in same ch-2 sp to the left of V-st, ch 3, [sc in next ch-1 sp between next 2 jdc, ch 3] rep across to next corner ch-2 sp **, sc in corner ch-2 sp to the right of first dc of V-st, rep from * around, ending last rep at **, join in beg sc, fasten off.

2nd Ruffle

Rep instructions for first ruffle on Rnd 21.

3rd Ruffle

Rep instructions for first ruffle on Rnd 28. ❖

Lullaby Crib Blanket

Design by Aline Suplinskas

A soft pink and variegated pastels give this pretty blanket lots of color with little effort!

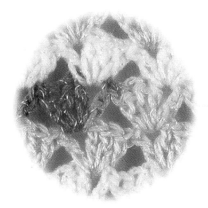

Skill Level
Intermediate

Size
32" x 41"

Materials
- Cuddlesoft Baby Pompadour yarn by Caron (1.75 oz per skein): 3 skeins each hey diddle #2828 (A), white #2801 (B), and baby pink #2807 (C)
- Size G/6 crochet hook or size needed to obtain gauge

Gauge
3 shells = 3" in patt st

Check gauge to save time.

Pattern Notes
Join rnds with a sl st unless otherwise stated.

Do not fasten off at end of each row. Carry colors not in use up edge of afghan until they are needed again.

To change color in dc, work last dc before color change until last 2 lps before final yo rem on hook, drop working color to WS, yo with next color, complete dc.

Pattern Stitches
Shell: [3 dc, ch 1, dc] in indicated st or sp.

Beg shell: Ch 3, [2 dc, ch 1, dc] in first ch-1 sp.

Afghan
Row 1 (RS): With A, ch 132 (foundation ch), ch 3 more (turning ch-3), [2 dc, ch 1, dc] in 4th ch from hook (beg shell made), [sk 3 chs, shell in next ch] rep across to last 3 chs, sk 2 chs, dc in last ch, changing to B, turn. (33 shells)

Row 2: Beg shell, [shell in next ch-1 sp] rep across, dc in 3rd ch of turning ch-3, changing to C, turn. (33 shells)

Row 3: With C, rep Row 2, changing to A in last st.

Rows 4–85: Rep Row 2 in the following color sequence: [1 row A, 1 row B, 1 row C] 27 times, ending with a Row A; at end of Row 85, fasten off.

Border
Rnd 1: With RS facing, attach B with a sl st over row end st at upper right corner, ch 1, [sc, ch 3 sc] in same sp, ch 1, sc in next ch-1 sp, [ch 1, sc in 2nd dc of next shell, ch 1, sc in next ch-1 sp] rep across to next corner, *ch 1, [sc, ch 3, sc] over row end st; working across side, ch 1, [sc over end st of next row, ch 1] rep across to last row *, [sc, ch 3, sc] over end st of last row; working in rem lps of foundation ch across, [ch 1, sc in next ch-3 sp, ch 1, sc at base of next shell] rep across to next corner, rep from * to *, join in beg sc, fasten off.

Continued on page 97

Spring Bouquet
Continued from page 80

Rnd 2: Sl st in first ch-5 sp, ch 4 (counts as first tr throughout), 4 tr in same sp, 5 dc in next sp, [5 tr in next sp, 5 dc in next sp] rep around, join in 4th ch of beg ch-4.

Rnd 3: Ch 4, tr in next tr, *5 tr in next tr **, tr in each of next 9 sts, rep from * around,

ending last rep at **, tr in each of next 7 sts, join in 4th ch of beg ch-4. (56 tr)

Rnd 4: Ch 3, [sk next tr, sl st in next tr, ch 3] rep around, join in same st as joining st of Rnd 3, fasten off.

Rem Squares (make 24)
Rnds 1–3: Rep Rnds 1–3 of first square with any flower B.

Joining Rnd
Rnd 4: [Ch 3, sk next tr, sl st in next tr] twice, [ch 1, sl st in center ch of next corresponding ch-3 on previous motif, ch 1, sk next tr on working motif, sl st in next tr] 7 times (1 side joined), continue around as for Rnd 4 of first square.

Following joining diagram for color placement, make and join 23 more squares in 5 rows of 5 squares each, joining on as many sides as are indicated on joining diagram.

Border
Rnd 1: With RS facing, attach A with a sl st in first ch-1 sp to the right of joining st between any corner square and next square, ch 1, sc in same sp, *[sc in next ch-1 sp, 3 hdc in next ch-3 sp, 3 dc in next ch-3 sp, 3 tr in next ch-3 sp, 5 tr in next ch-3 sp, 3 tr in next ch-3 sp, 3 dc in next ch-3 sp, 3 hdc in

next ch-3 sp, sc in next ch-1 sp] 3 times, sc in next ch-1 sp, 3 hdc in next sp, 3 dc in next sp, 3 tr in next sp, 5 tr in next sp, 3 tr in next sp, 3 dc in next sp, [dc, hdc, sc] in next sp, [sc, hdc, dc] in next sp, 3 dc in next sp, 3 tr in next sp, 5 tr in next sp, 3 tr in next sp, 3 dc in next sp, 3 hdc in next sp **, sc in next sp, rep from * around, ending last rep at *·, join in beg sc.

Rnd 2: Sl st in next sc, **[{ch 3, dc in same st, sk 2 sts, sl st in next st} 8 times, sl st in next sc] 3 times, *[ch 3, dc in same st, sk 2 sts, sl st in next st] 7 times *, ch 3, dc in same st, sk next st, sl st in each of next 2 sc, ch 3, dc in same st, sk next st, sl st in next st, rep from * to *, sl st in next st, rep from ** around, join in same st as joining st of Rnd 1, fasten off.

Fill-In Motif (make 16)
With RS facing, attach A with a sl st in first ch-1 sp before any joining st in sp between joining of any 4 squares, beg split pc, [split pc] 3 times, join between beg split pc and first split pc, fasten off.

Finishing
With sewing needle and white thread, tack center top of each petal on each flower to Rnd 2 of square directly behind it. ❖

Assembly Diagram

D	B	A	B	C
B	C	B	D	B
A	B	A	B	A
B	D	B	C	B
C	B	A	B	D

COLOR KEY
A Pastel green
B Pastel yellow
C Pastel blue
D Pastel pink

Sit Up Straight!
Always maintain good posture when crocheting. Keep elbows close to your body, and economize your movements as much as possible. Don't crochet while lying down; it is stressful on your elbows. Maintaining proper posture will help keep your arms and hands from getting tired and sore.

—Carli A. Damien

Practice, Practice, Practice
Before starting to crochet a project, practice holding the yarn and hook in

a comfortable manner that you will always use. Figuring a pattern takes time and patience, and it can all be for naught if your tension is not consistent. Uniform stitches make for a project that looks neat and professional, something you will be proud to display.

—Carli A. Damien

Finishing Touch
After weaving in the tails of yarn, I always sew them down with matching thread. This takes extra time, but it makes for a very finished look, a

"wrong" side that looks almost as good as the "right" side, and ends that almost never pop out.

—Katherine Eng

For a Smooth, Flat Finish
When making individual motifs and afghan borders, I often figure out a way to work one or two rounds with the wrong side facing. This prevents the motif design from twisting in one direction and prevents the border from curling up.

—Katherine Eng

Sweet Dreams

Continued from page 86

Assembly Diagram

D						A
Large Block MC/B	Small Block A MC/B	Small Block B MC/B	Small Block B MC/C	Small Block A MC/C	Large Block MC/C	
	Small Block B MC/B	Small Block A MC/B	Small Block A MC/C	Small Block B MC/C		
Small Block A MC/B	Small Block B MC/B	Large Block MC/B		Large Block MC/C	Small Block B MC/C	Small Block A MC/C
Small Block B MC/B	Small Block A MC/B				Small Block A MC/C	Small Block B MC/C
Small Block B MC/A	Small Block A MC/A	Large Block MC/A		Large Block MC/D	Small Block A MC/D	Small Block B MC/D
Small Block A MC/A	Small Block B MC/A				Small Block B MC/D	Small Block A MC/D
Large Block MC/A	Small Block B MC/A	Small Block A MC/A	Small Block A MC/D	Small Block B MC/D	Large Block MC/D	
	Small Block A MC/A	Small Block B MC/A	Small Block B MC/D	Small Block A MC/D		
C						B

Lullaby Crib Blanket

Continued from page 94

Rnd 2: With RS facing, attach C with a sl st in any corner ch-3 sp, ch 1, beg in same sp, *[sc, ch 3, sc] in corner sp, ch 1, [sc in next ch-1 sp, ch 1] rep across to next corner, rep from * around, join in beg sc.

Rnd 3: Sl st in first corner ch-3 sp, rep Rnd 2 from * around, fasten off. ❖

Just for Him

Treat the man of the house to a handsome afghan crocheted in his favorite colors. Whether he uses your hand-crocheted gift while watching television or relaxing in the den, he's sure to appreciate it!

Chapter 6

Woodland Skies

Design by Debby Caldwell

Your outdoors-loving husband will enjoy this tastefully-designed afghan featuring nature's most popular colors, blue and green!

Pattern Notes

Afghan is worked from side to side with 2 strands held tog throughout.

When attaching new colors at begs of rows and fastening off at ends of rows, leave 7" lengths to be worked into fringe.

Pattern Stitch

Long sc (lsc): Insert hook into next st in row before last, yo, draw up a lp to top of working row, complete sc.

Afghan

Row 1 (RS): With B, ch 116, sc in 2nd ch from hook and in each rem ch across, fasten off. (115 sc)

Row 2: With RS facing, attach C with a sl st in back lp only of first sc, ch 1, beg in same sc, sc in back lp only of each st across, fasten off. (115 sc)

Row 3: With RS facing, attach A with a sl st in back lp only of first sc, ch 1, sc in back lp only of same st and in each of next 3 sts, [lsc, sc in back lp only of each of next 4 sts] rep across to last st, sc in back lp only of last st, fasten off. (115 sts)

Row 4: With RS facing, attach E with

Skill Level

Intermediate

Size

42" x 52" excluding fringe

Materials

- Bernat Silky Soft worsted weight yarn (5 oz per skein): 6 skeins white #348 (A), 4 skeins each medium blue # 356 (B), light blue #354 (C), dark green #360 (D), and light green #358 (E), and 2 (4¼ oz) skeins moss lagoon #382 (F)
- Size P/16 crochet hook or size needed to obtain gauge

Gauge

9 sts = 4" in patt st with 2 strands held tog

Check gauge to save time.

a sl st in back lp only of first st, ch 1, sc in back lp only of same st and in each of next 2 sts, [lsc, sc in back lp only of each of next 4 sts] rep across to last 2 sts, lsc, sc in back lp only of last st, fasten off. (115 sts)

Row 5: With RS facing, attach D with a sl st in back lp only of first st, ch 1, sc in back lp only of same st and in next st, [lsc, sc in back lp only of each of

next 4 sts] rep across to last 3 sts, lsc in next sc, sc in back lp only of each of last 2 sts, fasten off. (115 sts)

Row 6: With RS facing, attach E with a sl st in back lp only of first st, ch 1, sc in back lp only of same st, [lsc, sc in back lp only of each of next 4 sts] rep across to last 4 sts, lsc in next st, sc in back lp only of each of next 3 sts, fasten off. (115 sc)

Row 7: With RS facing, attach A with a sl st in back lp only of first st, ch 1, sc in back lp only of same st, sc in back lp only of each of next 4 sts, [lsc, sc in back lp only of each of next 4 sts] rep across, fasten off. (115 sts)

Rows 8–93: Rep Rows 3–7 in the following color sequence, ending with a Row 3: [C, B, 5A, D, E, A, C, B, C, A, E, D, 5A, B, C, A, E, D, E, A] 3 times, C, B.

Row 94: With B, rep Row 2. (115 sc)

Fringe

Cut 8 (14") lengths of F. Holding all 8 strands tog, fold in half. Insert hook from WS to RS through end st of first row on either short edge of afghan, draw folded end through st on hook to form a lp, draw free ends, including 7" length left at beg or end of row, through lp. Pull to tighten. Rep in every other row across same edge. Rep in every other row end across opposite short edge. ❖

Autumn Chestnut

Design by Tammy C. Hildebrand

This beautiful afghan will remind you and yours of walking through a thick layer of leaves on a crisp autumn day!

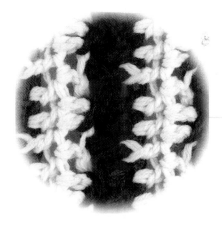

Skill Level
Intermediate

Size
52" x 74"

Materials
- Lion Brand Wool-Ease worsted weight yarn (3 oz per skein): 13 skeins fisherman #099 (MC), 7 skeins autumn #233 (A) and 4 skeins each forest green heather #180 (B) and chestnut heather #179 (C)
- Size P/16 crochet hook or size needed to obtain gauge

Gauge
8 dc = 4" holding 2 strands tog
Check gauge to save time.

Pattern Note
Afghan is worked from side to side holding 2 strands tog throughout.

Pattern Stitch
Crossed fpdc: Sk next unworked st, fpdc over next st, fpdc over sk st.

Afghan
Row 1 (RS): With MC, ch 153, dc in 4th ch from hook, dc in each rem ch across, fasten off, do not turn. (151 dc, counting last 3 chs of foundation ch as first dc)

Row 2: With RS facing, attach B with a sl st in first dc, ch 3 (counts as first dc throughout), [crossed fpdc, dc in next st] rep across, fasten off, do not turn. (50 crossed fpdc)

Row 3: With RS facing, attach A with a sl st in first dc, ch 3, dc in each of next 2 sts, [fpdc over next st, dc in each of next 2 sts] rep across, ending with dc in last st, fasten off, do not turn. (151 sts)

Row 4: With MC, rep Row 3; do not fasten off; turn.

Row 5: Ch 3, dc in each rem st across, fasten off, do not turn. (151 dc)

Row 6: With C, rep Row 2.

Row 7: Rep Row 3.

Rows 8 & 9: Rep Rows 4 and 5.

Rows 10–79: Rep Rows 2–9 alternately, ending with a Row 7.

Row 80: With RS facing, attach MC with a sl st in first st, ch 2 (counts as first hdc), hdc in each rem st across, fasten off. (151 hdc) ❖

Filet Ripple

Design courtesy of Spinrite

This shaded afghan can be crocheted to accent any decor. Simply match four shades of your living room's dominant color to create an afghan with a decorator's touch!

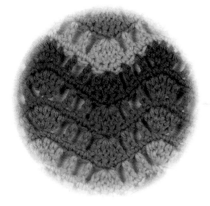

Pattern Stitches

Dc2tog: Holding back on hook last lp of each st, dc in each of next 2 sts, yo, draw through all 3 lps on hook.

Dc3tog: Holding back on hook last lp of each st, dc in each of next 3 sts, yo, draw through all 4 lps on hook.

Dc5tog: Holding back on hook last lp of each st, dc in each of next 5 sts, yo, draw through all 6 lps on hook.

Afghan

Row 1 (RS): With MC, ch 196, beg in 5th ch from hook, dc2tog, [ch 1, sk next ch, dc in next ch] twice, ch 1, sk next ch, *5 dc in next ch, [ch 1, sk next ch, dc in next ch] twice, ch 1, sk next ch **, dc5tog, [ch 1, sk next ch, dc in next ch] twice, ch 1, sk next ch, rep from * across to last 3 chs, ending last rep at **, dc3tog, ch 1, turn.

Row 2: Sc in each st and sp across, fasten off, turn. (193 sc)

Row 3: With RS facing, attach A with a sl st in first sc, ch 3 (counts as first dc throughout), dc2tog, [ch 1, sk next st, dc in next st] twice, ch 1, sk next st, *5 dc in next st, [ch 1, sk next st, dc in next st] twice, ch 1, sk next st **, dc5tog, [ch 1, sk next st, dc in next st] twice, ch 1, sk next st, rep from * across to last 3 sts, ending last rep at **, dc3tog, ch 1, turn.

Row 4: Rep Row 2.

Rows 5 & 6: With B, rep Rows 3 and 4.

Rows 7 & 8: With C, rep Rows 3 and 4.

Rows 9 & 10: With MC, rep Rows 3 and 4.

Rows 11 & 12: Rep Rows 3 and 4.

Rep Rows 5–12 consecutively until afghan meas approximately 56" from beg, ending with a Row 10; fasten off. ❖

Skill Level

Intermediate

Size

Approximately 46" x 56"

Materials

- Bernat Berella "4" worsted weight yarn (3.5 oz per skein): 3 skeins each dark ocean #8763 (MC), medium ocean #8762 (A), light ocean #8761 (B) and pale ocean #8760 (C)
- Size J/10 crochet hook or size needed to obtain gauge

Gauge

16 sts and 10 rows = 4" in pattern st
Check gauge to save time.

Natural Textures

Design by Maggie Weldon

Work this gorgeous afghan in a multi-hued textured yarn to create a lovely afghan that's soothing to the touch!

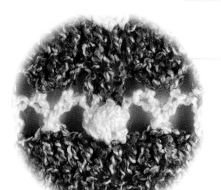

Pattern Note

Join rnds with a sl st unless otherwise stated.

Pattern Stitch

Cl: Holding back on hook last lp of each st, 4 dc in next st, yo, draw through all 5 lps on hook.

Afghan

Row 1(RS): With MC, ch 109, dc in 4th ch from hook, dc in each rem ch across, turn. (107 dc, counting last 3 chs of foundation ch as first dc)

Row 2: Ch 3 (counts as first dc throughout), dc in each rem st across, fasten off, turn. (107 dc)

Row 3: With RS facing, attach CC with a sl st in first st, ch 3, cl in next st, dc in next st, *ch 1, sk next 3 sts, dc in next st, ch 3, working in front of last dc made, sk next unworked st to the right, dc in next st (X-st made), ch 1, sk next st after first leg of X-st worked, dc in

Skill Level

Intermediate

Size

45" x 60" excluding fringe

Materials

- Lion Brand Homespun textured yarn (6 oz per skein): 6 skeins shaker #301 (MC) and 5 skeins hepplewhite #300 (CC)
- Size K/10-½ crochet hook or size needed to obtain gauge

Gauge

5 sts = 2" and 2 rows = 1½" in dc
Check gauge to save time.

next st, cl in next st, dc in next st, rep from * across, fasten off, do not turn. (13 X-sts)

Row 4: With RS facing, attach MC with a sl st in first st, ch 3, dc in each of next 2 sts, *5 dc in next ch-3 sp, sk next sp, dc in each of next 3 sts, rep from * across, turn. (107 dc)

Rep Rows 2–4 alternately until afghan meas 60" or desired length, ending with a Row 2, fasten off.

Border

Rnd 1: With RS facing, attach MC with a sl st in upper right-hand corner, ch 1, 2 sc in same st, sc in each rem st across to next corner, 3 sc in last st; *working over ends of rows, sc evenly sp across to next corner *, working in rem lps across opposite side of foundation ch, 3 sc in first st, sc across to next corner, 3 sc in last st, rep from * to *, sc in same st as beg sc, join in beg sc.

Rnd 2: Ch 1, [sc, ch 3, sc] in same st as joining, *ch 3, [sk next st, sc in next st, ch 3] rep across to next corner **, adjusting number of sts sk before corner, if necessary, to work [sc, ch 3, sc] in corner st, rep from * around, ending last rep at **, join in beg sc, fasten off.

Fringe

Cut 4 (10") lengths of CC. Holding all 4 strands tog, fold in half. Insert hook from WS to RS in first ch-3 sp across either short edge of afghan. Pull folded end of strands through sp to form a lp, draw free ends through lp, pull to tighten. Rep for each rem ch-3 sp across same edge and for each ch-3 sp across opposite short edge. ❖

Southwest Sunset

Design by Maggie Weldon

Whether you live in the Southwest or simply enjoy a decor rich with shades of gold, you'll enjoy cuddling up under this afghan.

Pattern Notes

Join rnds with a sl st unless otherwise stated.

Afghan is worked holding 2 strands tog throughout.

Pattern Stitches

Shell: 5 tr in indicated st.

Half shell: 3 tr in indicated st.

Beg half shell: [Ch 4, 2 tr] in indicated st.

Afghan

Row 1 (RS): With MC, ch 92, sc in 2nd ch from hook, [sk 2 chs, shell in next ch, sk 2 chs, sc in next ch] rep across, turn. (15 shells)

Row 2: Beg half shell in first st, sc in center tr of next shell, [shell in next st, sc in center tr of next shell] rep across to last shell, half shell in last sc, fasten off. (14 shells, 2 half shells)

Row 3: With RS facing, attach CC with a sl st in first st, ch 1, sc in same

Skill Level

Intermediate

Size

47" x 62"

Materials

- Patons Canadiana worsted weight yarn (3-oz per skein): 14 (3-oz) skeins high plains #434 (MC) and 5 (3½-oz) skeins gold #81 (CC)
- Size Q crochet hook or size needed to obtain gauge

Gauge

Shell = 2¾" with 2 strands held tog
Check gauge to save time.

st, shell in next sc, [sc in center tr of next shell, shell in next sc] rep across to last sc, sc in last sc, fasten off. (15 shells)

Row 4: With RS facing, attach MC with a sl st in first sc, rep Row 2; do not fasten off; turn.

Row 5: Ch 1, sc in first st, shell in next sc, [sc in center tr of next shell, shell in

next sc] rep across to last sc, sc in 4th ch of turning ch-4, fasten off.

Row 6: With RS facing, attach CC with a sl st in first sc, rep Row 2.

Row 7: With MC, rep Row 3; do not fasten off; turn.

Row 8: Rep Row 2.

Rows 9–62: Rep Rows 3–8 alternately; at end of Row 62, do not fasten off; ch 1, turn.

Border

Rnd 1: 3 sc in first st, sc in each of next 2 tr, hdc in next sc, [sc in each of next 5 tr, hdc in next sc] rep across to last sc, sc in each of next 2 tr, 3 sc in last st; *working over ends of rows across, work 123 more sc evenly sp across to next corner *; working in rem lps of foundation ch across, 3 sc in first st, sc in each rem st across to last st, 3 sc in last st, rep from * to *, join in beg sc.

Rnd 2: Sl in next sc, ch 4 (counts as first hdc, ch-2), hdc in same st, *ch 1, [sk next st, hdc in next st, ch 1] rep across to next corner **, [hdc, ch 2, hdc] in corner st, rep from * around, ending last rep at **, join in beg sc, fasten off. ❖

Ever-Green Afghan

Design by Connie L. Folse

This extra-long afghan will quickly become your husband's favorite. With its long length and soft feel, he'll stay cozy from head to toe!

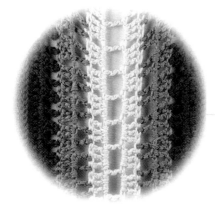

Pattern Notes

Join rnds with a sl st unless otherwise stated.

Afghan is worked holding 3 strands tog throughout.

Pattern Stitch

Treble tr (trtr): Yo 4 times, insert hook in indicated st or sp, yo, draw up a lp, [yo, draw through 2 lps on hook] 5 times.

Panel (make 4)

Row 1 (RS): With C, ch 135 (foundation ch), ch 6 more (counts as first tr, ch-2), tr in 9th ch from hook, [ch 2, sk 2 chs, tr in next ch] rep across. (45 ch-2 sps)

Rnd 2: Sl st into first sp, ch 4 (counts as first tr throughout), 7 tr in same sp, *[3 tr in next sp] 43 times *, 12 tr over last sp; working down opposite side of Row 1, rep from * to *, 4 tr in same st as beg ch-4, join in 4th ch of beg ch-4, fasten off. (282 tr)

Rnd 3: With RS facing, attach B with a sl st in joining st, ch 7 (counts as first tr, ch-3), sk 2 tr, [tr in next tr, ch 3, sk 2 tr] rep around, join in 4th ch of beg ch-7. (94 ch-3 sps)

Rnd 4: Ch 4, *tr in next ch-3 sp, trtr in 2nd of next 2 sk tr of rnd before last, tr in same ch-3 sp as last tr made **, tr in next tr, rep from * around, ending last rep at **, join in 4th ch of beg ch-4, fasten off. (376 sts)

Rnd 5: With RS facing, attach A with a sl st in same st as joining, ch 4, tr in same st, ch 3, sk 3 sts, [2 tr in next st, ch 3, sk next 3 sts] rep around, join in 4th ch of beg ch-4.

Rnd 6: Ch 4, tr in next st, *tr in next ch-3 sp, trtr in center st of next group of 3 sk sts on rnd before last, tr in same ch-3 sp as last tr made **, tr in each of next 2 tr, rep from * around, ending last rep at **, join in 4th ch of beg ch-4, fasten off.

Assembly

Holding 2 panels with RS tog, working through both thicknesses in back lps only, sl st across 212 sts along straight edge, fasten off. Rep with rem panels. ❖

Skill Level

Intermediate

Size

Approximately 66" x 94"

Materials

- Red Heart Soft worsted weight yarn (5 oz per skein): 12 skeins dark blue green #7665 (A), 6 skeins light blue green #7664 (B) and 5 skeins aran #7018 (C)
- Size N/15 crochet hook or size needed to obtain gauge

Gauge

2 tr = 1" with 3 strands held tog

Check gauge to save time.

Navy & Cream Throw

Design by Tammy C. Hildebrand

Select Dad's favorite color and work it with off-white to create this treat to the eyes as well as the body!

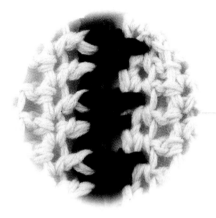

Skill Level

Intermediate

Size

47" x 68" excluding fringe

Materials

- Lion Brand Wool-Ease worsted weight yarn (3 oz per skein): 15 skeins fisherman #099 (MC) and 10 skeins navy #111 (CC)
- Size Q crochet hook or size needed to obtain gauge

Gauge

7 dc = 5" with 3 strands held tog

Check gauge to save time.

Pattern Note

Afghan is worked from side to side, holding 3 strands tog throughout.

Afghan

Row 1 (WS): With MC ch 97, dc in 4th ch from hook, dc in each rem ch across, ch 1, turn. (95 dc)

Row 2: Sc in first st, [ch 1, sk next st, sc in next st] rep across, fasten off, turn.

Row 3: With WS facing, attach CC with a sl st in first sc, ch 3 (counts as first dc throughout), [tr over ch-1 sp into next st of row before last, dc in next sc] rep across, fasten off, turn. (95 sts)

Row 4: With RS facing, attach MC with a sl st in first dc, ch 3, [fpdc over next st, dc in next st] rep across, turn. (95 sts)

Row 5: Ch 3, dc in each st across, ch 1, turn. (95 dc)

Rows 6 & 7: Rep Rows 2 and 3.

Rows 8–49: Rep Rows 4–7 alternately, ending with a Row 5; at end of Row 49, fasten off.

Edging

With RS facing, working across either short edge, attach MC with a sl st over end st of first row at right-hand edge, ch 1, beg in same st, [sc, ch 1] evenly sp over row ends across to next corner, ending with sc in corner st, fasten off.

Rep across opposite short edge.

Fringe

Cut 10 (20") lengths of CC for first ch-1 sp on either short edge. Holding all strands tog, fold in half. Insert hook from WS to RS in ch-1 sp, draw folded end of strands through sp to form lp, draw free ends through lp, and pull to tighten. Rep for each rem ch-1 sp across same edge and across opposite short edge. ❖

Tweed Ripple

Design by Laura Gebhardt

Pick your father's favorite colors for this eye-catching afghan. It's just right for keeping dad warm in style!

Pattern Stitches

Dc5tog: Holding back on hook last lp of each st, dc in each of next 5 sts, yo, draw through all 6 lps on hook.

Dc3tog: Holding back on hook last lp of each st, dc in each of next 3 sts, yo, draw through all 4 lps on hook.

Beg dc3tog: Ch 2, dc dec over next 2 sts.

Split dc3tog (sp dc3tog): Holding back on hook last lp of each st, dc in each of next 2 sts, sk next st, dc in 2nd ch of turning ch-2, yo, draw through all 4 lps on hook.

Afghan

Row 1 (RS): With 1 strand A and 1 strand B held tog, ch 140 (foundation ch), ch 2 more (turning ch), dc dec over 3rd ch from hook and next ch (beg dc3tog made), dc in each of next 11 chs, 5 dc in next ch, dc in each of next 11 chs, [dc5tog, dc in each of next 11 chs, 5 dc in next ch, dc in each of next 11 chs] rep across to last 3 chs, dc3tog, turn.

Row 2: Working in back lps only across, beg dc3tog, dc in each of next 11 sts, 5 dc in next st, dc in each of next 11 sts, [dc5tog, dc in each of next 11 sts, 5 dc in next st, dc in each of next 11 sts] rep across to last 4 sts, sp dc3tog, turn.

Rows 3–10: Rep Row 2; at end of Row 10, fasten off A.

Rows 11 & 12: With 2 strands B held tog, rep Row 2; at end of Row 12, fasten off 1 strand B.

Rows 13–16: With 1 strand A and 1 strand B held tog, rep Row 2; at end of Row 16, fasten off B.

Rows 17 & 18: With 2 strands A held tog, rep Row 2; at end of Row 18, fasten off 1 strand A.

Rows 19–38: With 1 strand A and 1 strand B held tog, rep Row 2; at end of Row 38, fasten off B.

Rows 39 & 40: With 2 strands A held tog, rep Row 2; at end of Row 40, fasten off 1 strand A.

Rows 41–44: With 1 strand A and 1 strand B held tog, rep Row 2; at end of Row 44, fasten off A.

Rows 45 & 46: With 2 strands B held tog, rep Row 2; at end of Row 46, fasten off 1 strand B.

Rows 47–56: With 1 strand A and 1 strand B held tog, rep Row 2; at end of Row 56, fasten off.

Edging

With RS facing, working over ends of rows across, attach 1 strand A and 1 strand B held tog with a sl st at right-hand edge of either long edge, ch 1, beg in same st, sc evenly sp over ends of rows across to next corner, ch 1, do not turn, rev sc across, fasten off.

Rep edging across opposite long edge. ❖

Skill Level

Intermediate

Size

Approximately 46" x 69"

Materials

- Coats & Clark Red Heart Super Saver worsted weight yarn (8 oz per skein): 4 skeins each black #312 (A) and burgundy #376 (B)
- Size N/15 crochet hook or size needed to obtain gauge

Gauge

10 dc = 4" with 2 strands held tog
Check gauge to save time.

Ripple Rhapsody

Design by Darla J. Fanton

Ripple Rhapsody features cascades of beautiful colors worked in a ravishing ripple pattern. It makes a lovely addition to a sunroom or bedroom.

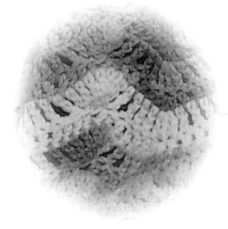

Skill Level
Intermediate

Size
55" x 72"

Materials
- Bernat® Berella "4"® worsted weight yarn: 33½ oz meadow variegated #8967 (MC) and 16½ oz pale lagoon #8819 (CC)
- Size J/10 crochet hook or size needed to obtain gauge

Gauge
3 dc = 1"

Check gauge to same time.

Pattern Stitches
Beg 3-tr cl: Ch 3, holding back on hook last lp of each st, tr in each of next 2 sts, yo, draw through all 3 lps on hook.

3-tr cl: Holding back on hook last lp of each st, tr in each of next 3 indicated sts, yo, draw through all 4 lps on hook.

7-tr cl: Holding back on hook last lp of each st, tr in each of next 7 sts, yo, draw through all 8 lps on hook.

Afghan
Row 1: With MC, ch 193, holding back on hook last lp of each st, tr in 4th ch from hook and in next ch, yo, draw through all 3 lps on hook, *[ch 1, tr in next ch] 4 times, ch 1, 3 tr in next ch, [ch 1, tr in next ch] 4 times, ch 1 **, 7-tr cl over next 7 chs, rep from * across, ending last rep at **, 3-tr cl over last 3 chs, turn.

Row 2: Ch 3 (counts as first dc throughout), dc in each of next 5 tr, *3 dc in next tr, dc in each of next 4 tr **, dc in next ch-1 sp, dc in next tr, sk 7-tr cl, dc in next ch-1 sp, dc in next tr, dc in next ch-1 sp, dc in each of next 4 tr, rep from * across, ending last rep at **, dc in next tr, dc in top of beg 3-tr cl, turn.

Row 3: Beg 3-tr cl, *[ch 1, tr in next dc] 4 times, ch 1, 3 tr in next dc, [ch 1, tr in next dc] 4 times, ch 1 **, 7-tr cl over next 7 dc, rep from * across, ending last rep at **, 3-tr cl over last 3 sts, turn.

Rep Rows 2 and 3, working 4 rows of MC and 2 rows of CC, ending when piece meas approximately 72" or desired length after 4th row of MC stripe, fasten off at end of last row.

Weave in loose ends. ❖

Christmas Traditions

*Y*ou'll find many uses for this collection of festive Christmas afghans throughout the holiday season, from covering your little ones as they wait for Santa to snuggling up with your sweetie after a night of wrapping gifts!

Chapter 7

Victorian Christmas

Design by Laura Gebhardt

Wrap yourself in elegance this holiday season with this beautiful afghan worked in shades of antique rose.

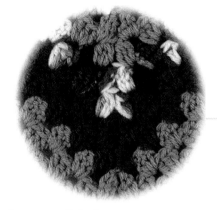

Skill Level
Intermediate

Size
Approximately 40" x 52"

Materials
- Red Heart Classic worsted weight yarn: 2 (8 oz) skeins light sage #631 (MC), 1 (8 oz) skein dark sage #633 (A), and 1 (6 oz) skein holly and ivy #967 (B)
- Size 8/H crochet hook or size needed to obtain gauge

Gauge
Three 3-dc groups = $2\frac{1}{2}$" in pattern st
Check gauge to save time.

Pattern Stitch
Cl: Holding back on hook last lp of each st, work 3 dc in indicated st or sp, yo, draw through all 4 lps on hook.

Afghan
Row 1: With A, ch 187, sc in 2nd ch from hook and in each rem ch across, turn. (186 sc)

Row 2: Ch 3 (counts as first dc throughout), [sk next 2 sc, 3 dc in next sc] 3 times, *sk 2 sc, [3 dc, ch 3, 3 dc] in next sc, [sk 2 sc, 3 dc in next sc] twice, sk 2 sc **, cl in next sc, sk 4 sc, cl in next sc, [sk 2 sc, 3 dc in next sc] twice, rep from * across to last 4 sc, ending last rep at **, 3 dc in next sc, sk 2 sc, dc in last sc, turn.

Row 3: Ch 3, [3 dc between next 2 3-dc groups] 3 times, *[3 dc, ch 3, 3 dc] in next ch-3 sp, [3 dc between next 2 3-dc groups] twice **, cl between next 3-dc group and next cl, cl between next cl and next 3-dc group, [3 dc between next two 3-dc groups] twice, rep from * across, ending last rep at **, 3 dc between next two 3-dc groups, dc in 3rd ch of turning ch-3, fasten off, turn.

Row 4: Attach B with a sl st in top of first dc, rep Row 3; do not fasten off; turn.

Row 5: Ch 3, [3 dc between next two 3-dc groups] 3 times, *[3 dc, ch 3, 3 dc] in next ch-3 sp, [3 dc between next two 3-dc groups] twice **, cl between next 3 dc-group and next cl, cl between next cl and next 3-dc groups, [3 dc between next two 3-dc groups] twice, rep from * across, ending last rep at **, 3 dc between next two 3-dc groups, dc in 3rd ch of turning ch-3, turn.

Rows 6 & 7: Rep Row 5; at end of Row 7, fasten off, turn.

Row 8: With MC, rep Row 4.

Row 9: Rep Row 3.

Row 10: Rep Row 4.

Row 11: Rep Row 3.

Row 12: With A, rep Row 4.

Row 13: Rep Row 3.

Row 14: Rep Row 8.

Rows 15–64: Rep Row 5; at end of Row 64, fasten off, turn.

Rows 65 & 66: Rep Rows 12 and 13.

Rows 67 & 68: Rep Rows 10 and 11.

Rows 69 & 70: Rep Rows 8 and 9.

Rows 71–74: Rep Rows 4–7.

Rows 75 & 76: Rep Rows 12 and 13. ❖

Candy Cane Throw

Design by Tammy C. Hildebrand

Most candy canes are made to be eaten, but these candy cane panels are made to be snuggled in!

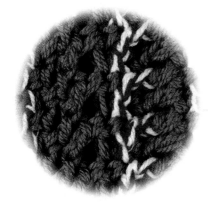

Skill Level
Intermediate

Size
42" x 54"

Materials
- Worsted weight yarn: 48 oz green, 8 oz each red and white
- Size P/16 crochet hook or size needed to obtain gauge

Gauge
7 dc = 3" with 2 strands held tog
Check gauge to save time.

Pattern Note
Join rnds with a sl st unless otherwise stated.

Pattern Stitch
Joining sp (jsp): Ch 1, remove hook from lp, insert hook in center ch of corresponding ch-3 on previous panel, pick up dropped lp and draw through st on hook, ch 1.

First Panel
Rnd 1 (RS): With 2 strands green held tog, ch 103 (foundation ch), ch 3 more (beg ch-3), [dc, ch 3, 2 dc] in 4th ch from hook, dc in each rem ch across to last ch, [2 dc, ch 3, 2 dc] in last ch; working in rem lps across opposite side of foundation ch, dc in each rem st across, join in 3rd ch of beg ch-3, fasten off. (210 dc, counting beg ch-3 as first dc)

Rnd 2: With RS facing, attach 1 strand red and 1 strand white held tog with a sl st in either end ch-3 sp, ch 3 (counts as first dc throughout), [dc, ch 2, 3 dc, ch 2, 2 dc] in same sp, *fpdc over next dc, [ch 1, sk next dc, fpdc over next dc] rep across to next ch-3 sp *, [2 dc, ch 2, 3 dc, ch 2, 2 dc] in ch-3

sp, rep from * to *, join in 3rd ch of beg ch-3, fasten off. (14 dc, 106 fpdc)

Rnd 3: With RS facing, attach 2 strands green held tog with a sl st in first end ch-2 sp to the right at either end of panel, ch 1, beg in same sp, *[3 sc, ch 2, 3 sc] in ch-2 sp, ch 1, sk next dc, sc in next dc, ch 1, [3 sc, ch 2, 3 sc] in next ch-2 sp, sc in each of next 2 dc and in next fpdc, [working behind ch-1 sp, dc in next sk st of rnd before last, sc in next fpdc] rep across to opposite end, sc in each of next 2 dc before first end ch-2 sp, rep from * around, join in beg sc.

Rnd 4: Sl st in next sc, ch 3, *[2 dc, ch 3, 2 dc] in next sp, sk 2 sts, tr in next st, [sk ch-1 sp, tr in next st] twice, [2 dc, ch 3, 2 dc] in next sp, sk next st, dc in next st, sk next st, dc in each of next 109 sts, sk next st**, dc in next st, rep from * around, ending last rep at **, join in 3rd ch of beg ch-3, fasten off.

Continued on page 138

Holly Berry Throw

Design by Margret Willson

Deck the halls with boughs of holly and accent your living room with this festive afghan!

Pattern Notes

Join rnds with a sl st unless otherwise stated.

Afghan is worked from side to side.

Pattern Stitches

V-st: [Dc, ch 1, dc] in indicated st or sp.

Tr5tog: Holding back on hook last lp of each st, tr in each of next 5 dc, yo, draw through all 6 lps on hook.

Afghan

Row 1 (RS): With MC, ch 196 (foundation ch), ch 3 more (turning ch-3), V-st in 6th ch from hook, [sk 2 chs, V-st in next ch] rep across to last ch, dc in last ch, turn. (65 V-sts)

Row 2: Ch 3 (counts as first dc throughout), V-st in each V-st sp across, dc in 3rd ch of turning ch-3, fasten off. (65 V-sts)

Row 3: With RS facing, attach B with a sl st in first dc, ch 1, sc in same st, sc in each dc and ch-1 sp across, ending with sc in 3rd ch of turning ch-3, fasten off. (197 sc)

Row 4: With WS facing, attach A with a sl st in first sc, ch 3, sk next 2 sc, 5 dc in next sc, [sk 4 sc, 5 dc in next sc] rep across to last 3 sc, sk 2 sc, dc in last sc,

Skill Level

Intermediate

Size

Approximately 42" x 56" including border

Materials

- Worsted weight yarn: 15 oz white (MC)
- Victorian Gold Christmas worsted weight yarn (1.75 oz per skein): 7 skeins dark cranberry #1900 (A) and 6 skeins dark balsam green #1901 (B)
- Size H/8 crochet hook or size needed to obtain gauge

Gauge

6 V-sts = 4½" in pattern st

Check gauge to save time.

turn. (39 5-dc groups)

Row 5: Ch 5 (counts as first dc, ch-2), tr5tog, [ch 4, tr5tog] rep across to last 5-dc group, ch 2, dc in 3rd ch of turning ch-3, fasten off.

Row 6: With RS facing, attach B with a sl st in 3rd ch of turning ch-5, ch 1, sc in same st, 2 sc in next ch-2 sp, sc in top of next tr5tog, [4 sc in next ch-4 sp, sc in top of next tr5tog] rep across to ch-2 sp, 2 sc in ch-2 sp, sc in last dc, fasten off. (197 sc)

Row 7: With WS facing, attach MC with a sl st in first sc, ch 3, sk 2 sc, [V-st in next sc, sk 2 sc] rep across to last sc, dc in last sc, turn.

Row 8: Rep Row 2.

Row 9: With RS facing, attach B with a sl st in 3rd ch of turning ch-3, ch 1, sc in same st, sc in each dc and ch-1 sp across, fasten off.

Rows 10–12: Rep Rows 7–9.

Rows 13–80: Rep Rows 4–12 alternately, ending with a Row 8.

Border

Rnd 1: With RS facing, attach B with a sl st in first st at right corner of last row, ch 1, 2 sc in same st, sc in each st and each sp across to next corner, *3 sc in corner st; working across short edge, work sc over end st of each sc row and 2 dc over end st of all other rows across to next corner *, 3 sc in corner st; working across foundation ch, work sc in rem lp at base of each V-st and 2 sc in each ch-2 sp across to next corner, rep from * to *, sc in same st as beg sc, join in beg sc, fasten off.

Rnd 2: With RS facing, attach A with a sl st in any sc, ch 1, sc in same st, sc in each st around, working 3 sc in each corner st, join in beg sc, fasten off.

Rnd 3: With MC, rep Rnd 2.

Rnd 4: With B, rep Rnd 2.

Rnd 5: Rep Rnd 2. ❖

Christmas Confetti

Design by Beverly Mewhorter

Wrap your youngsters up in this warm afghan after a delightful evening of family Christmas caroling!

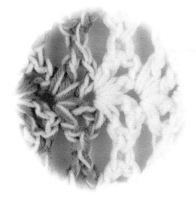

Pattern Stitch

Shell: [{Dc, ch 1} 3 times, dc] in indicated st or sp.

Afghan

Row 1 (RS): With 1 strand A and 1 strand B held tog, ch 100 (foundation ch), ch 3 more (turning ch-3), shell in 7th ch from hook, [sk 3 chs, shell in next ch] rep across to last 4 chs, sk 3 chs, dc in last ch, turn. (24 shells; 1 dc at each edge, counting turning ch-3 as first dc)

Row 2: Ch 3 (counts as first dc throughout), [shell in center sp of next shell] rep across, dc in 3rd ch of turning ch-3, turn.

Rows 3–7: Rep Row 2; at end of Row 7, fasten off B, turn.

Rows 8–10: With 2 strands A held tog, rep Row 2; at end of Row 10, fasten off 1 strand A, turn.

Rows 11–17: With 1 strand A and 1 strand C held tog, rep Row 2; at end of Row 17, fasten off C, turn.

Rows 18–20: Rep Rows 8–10.

Rows 21–27: With 1 strand A and 1 strand B held tog, rep Row 2; at end of Row 27, fasten off B, turn.

Skill Level

Intermediate

Size

44" x 51" excluding fringe

Materials

- Worsted weight yarn: 30 oz white (A), 14 oz green (B), and 10 oz red (C)
- Size N/15 crochet hook or size needed to obtain gauge

Gauge

Shell = 2⅛" with 2 strands held tog
Check gauge to save time.

Rows 28–47: Rep Rows 8–27; at end of Row 47, do not fasten off B; ch 1, turn.

Row 48: Sc in first st, ch 3, [sc in center sp of next shell, ch 3] rep across, sc in 3rd ch of turning ch-3, fasten off.

Fringe

Cut 3 (12") lengths of B. Holding all 3 strands tog, fold in half. Insert hook from WS to RS through end st of Row 1, draw folded end of strands through end st to form lp, draw free ends through lp, pull to tighten. Rep with 3 more strands B through end st of same row. Working with 12" strands of B for all rows that contain B, C for all rows that contain C, and A for all rows that contain double strand of A, work 2 (3-strand) groups of fringe for each rem row across same short edge; rep across opposite short edge. ❖

Cozy Christmas

Design by Tammy C. Hildebrand

Crocheted with faux mohair yarn, this oh-so-soft afghan will enjoy much use during the entire holiday season!

Skill Level

Intermediate

Size

Approximately 37" x 63" excluding fringe

Materials

- Lion Brand Jiffy mohair-look yarn (3 oz per ball): 9 balls white #100 (A), 4 balls each forest green #131 (B) and wine #189 (C)
- Size Q crochet hook or size needed to obtain gauge

Gauge

3 dc = 2" with 2 strands held tog

Check gauge to save time.

Pattern Note

Afghan is worked with 2 strands held tog throughout.

Afghan

Row 1 (RS): With A, ch 57, dc in 4th ch from hook, dc in each rem ch across, fasten off. (55 dc, counting last 3 chs of foundation ch as first dc)

Row 2: With RS facing, attach B with a sl st in 3rd ch of beg ch-3, ch 4 (counts as first dc, ch-1 throughout), sk next st, dc in next st, [ch 1, sk next st, dc in next st] rep across, fasten off.

Row 3: With RS facing, attach A with a sl st in 3rd ch of beg ch-4, sc in same st, [working behind next ch-1 sp, dc in next sk st of row before last, sc in next dc on working row] rep across, fasten off.

Row 4: With RS facing, attach C with a sl st in first sc, ch 4, sk next st, dc in next st, [ch 1, sk next st, dc in next st] rep across, fasten off.

Row 5: Rep Row 3.

Row 6: With B, rep Row 4.

Rows 7–89: Rep Rows 3–6 alternately, ending with a Row 5; do not fasten off at end of Row 89; turn.

Row 90: Ch 3, dc in each rem st across, fasten off.

Fringe

Cut 2 (16") lengths of each color. Holding all 6 strands tog, fold in half, insert hook from WS to RS in first st across either short edge, draw folded end of strands through st to form a lp, pull free ends of strands through lp, pull to tighten. Rep for each rem st across same edge and each st across opposite short edge. ❖

Six-Hour Granny

Design by Christina McNeese

Here's an afghan that makes a wonderful last-minute gift for a special someone! It takes just six hours to crochet from start to finish!

Pattern Notes

Join rnds with a sl st unless otherwise stated.

Afghan is worked with 2 strands held tog throughout.

Motif (make 12)

Rnd 1 (RS): With C, ch 6, join to form a ring, ch 3 (counts as first dc throughout), 15 dc in ring, join in 3rd ch of beg ch-3, fasten off. (16 dc)

Rnd 2: With RS facing, attach B with a sl st in any dc, ch 3, 2 dc in same st as joining, sk next dc, [3 dc in next dc, sk next dc] rep around, join in 3rd ch of beg ch-3, fasten off. (8 3-dc groups)

Rnd 3: With RS facing, attach A with a sl st between any 2 3-dc groups, ch 3, 4 dc in same sp, [5 dc between next 2 3-dc groups] rep around, join in 3rd ch of beg ch-3, fasten off. (8 5-dc groups)

Rnd 4: With RS facing, attach MC with a sl st in first dc to the right on any 5-dc group, ch 3, *dc in each of next 2 sts, tr in each of next 2 sts, ch 3, tr in each of next 2 sts, dc in each of next 3 sts **, dc in first dc of next 5-dc group, rep from * around, ending last rep at **, join in 3rd ch of beg ch-3, fasten off.

Rnd 5: With RS facing, attach B with a sl st in first st to the left of any corner ch-3 sp, ch 1; beg in same st, [sc in each st across to next corner ch-3 sp, ch 3, sk corner ch-3 sp] rep around, join in beg

Skill Level

Intermediate

Size

Approximately 45" x 57" including border

Materials

- Worsted weight yarn (5 oz per ball): 6 balls claret (MC), 4 balls each Christmas (A), Christmas green (B), and white (C)
- Size K/10½ crochet hook or size needed to obtain gauge

Gauge

Rnds 1 and 2 = 6¼" in diameter with 2 strands held tog.

Check gauge to save time.

sc, fasten off. (40 sc)

Rnd 6: With RS facing, working over ch-3 sp of Rnd 5, attach MC with a sl st in any corner ch-3 sp of Rnd 4, ch 7 (counts as first tr, ch-3), tr in same sp, *dc in each st across to next corner ch-3 sp **; working over ch-3 sp of Rd 5, [tr, ch 3, tr] in ch-3 sp of Rnd 4, rep from * around, ending last rep at **, join in 4th ch of beg ch-7, fasten off.

Assembly

With RS tog, sc motifs tog with MC in 4 rows of 3 motifs each.

Border

Rnd 1: With RS facing, attach MC with a sl st in any ch-3 sp, ch 1, beg in same sp, [5 sc in corner ch-3 sp, sc evenly sp across to next corner] rep around, join in beg sc, fasten off.

Rnd 2: With RS facing, attach A with a sl st in center sc of any 5-sc corner group, ch 1, sc in same st, *sk 2 sts, [3 tr, ch 3, 3 tr] in next st, sk 2 sts, sc in next st, rep from * across to next corner, adjusting number of sts sk before corner if necessary to end with sc in center sc of 5-sc corner group, rep from * around, join in beg sc, fasten off. ❖

Cranberry Ripple

Design by Katherine Eng

Soft shades of rose and sage give this Christmas afghan a subtle, yet enchanting, holiday look.

Pattern Note

Join rnds with a sl st unless otherwise stated.

Pattern Stitches

Shell: [3 dc, ch 2, 3 dc] in indicated st or sp.

Beg dc dec: Ch 2, dc in next sc.

Afghan

Row 1 (RS): With B, ch 138, sc in 2nd ch from hook, [sk 3 chs, shell in next ch, sk 3 chs, sc in next ch] rep across, fasten off, turn. (17 shells)

Row 2: Attach A with a sl st in first sc, ch 1, sc dec over same st and first dc of next shell, sc in each of next 2 dc, *[sc, ch 2, sc] in shell sp **, sc in each of next 3 dc, sk next sc, sc in each of next 3 dc, rep from * across, ending last rep at **, sc in each of next 2 dc, sc dec over next dc and next sc, ch 1, turn.

Row 3: Sc dec, sc in each of next 2 sc, *[sc, ch 2, sc] in next ch-2 sp **, sc in each of next 3 sc, sk 2 sc, sc in each of next 3 sc, rep from * across, ending last rep at **, sc in each of next 2 sc, sc dec, ch 1, turn.

Row 4: Rep Row 3; fasten off, turn.

Skill Level

Intermediate

Size

42" x 62" including border

Materials

- Red Heart Super Saver worsted weight yarn: 3 (6 oz) skeins holly and ivy #967 (A), 2 (8 oz) skeins medium sage #632 (B), and 1 (8 oz) skein light sage #631 (C)
- Size J/10 crochet hook or size needed to obtain gauge

Gauge

Shell = 2"

Check gauge to save time.

Row 5: Attach B with a sl st in first st, beg dc dec, 2 dc in same st as last leg of dc dec, *sk 2 sc, sc in next ch-2 sp, sk 2 sc **, 3 dc in next sc, ch 2, sk 2 sc, 3 dc in next sc, rep from * across, ending last rep at **, 2 dc in next sc, sc dec over same sc and last st, ch 1, turn.

Row 6: Sc in first st, sk 2 dc, *shell in next sc **, sk 3 dc, sc in next ch-2 sp, sk 3 dc, rep from * across, ending last rep at **, sk 2 dc, sc in top of beg dc dec, fasten off, turn.

Rows 7–19: Rep Rows 2–6 alternately, ending with a Row 4.

Rows 20 & 21: With C, rep Rows 5 & 6.

Rows 22–119: Rep Rows 2–21 alternately, ending with a Row 19.

Continued on page 139

Christmas Stripes

Design by Dot Drake

*Children will love the festive stripes on this
very merry Christmas afghan!*

Skill Level

Intermediate

Size

Approximately 40" x 70" not
including fringe

Materials

- Bulky weight yarn: 30 oz red,
  20 oz each green and white
- Size N/15 crochet hook or size
  needed to obtain gauge

Gauge

[Sc, ch 3, 3 dc] twice in pattern st
= 4$\frac{1}{2}$"

Check gauge to save time.

Pattern Note

Afghan is worked from side to side.

Pattern Stitches

Dc2tog: Holding back on hook last lp
of each st, dc in each of next 2 sts, yo,
draw through all 3 lps on hook.

Cl: Holding back on hook last lp of
each st, 2 dc in indicated sp, yo, draw
through all 3 lps on hook.

Afghan

Row 1 (RS): With red, ch 176 (foundation ch), ch 3 more (turning ch-3), dc in
4th ch from hook, dc in each of next 2
chs, *ch 1, sk 2 chs, sc in next ch, ch 3 **,
dc in each of next 3 chs, rep from * across
to last 2 chs, ending last rep at **, dc2tog
over last 2 chs, turn. (29 3-dc groups)

Row 2: Ch 3, 3 dc in first ch-3 sp, *ch
1, sc in 3rd ch of next ch-3, ch 3, 3 dc in
same sp, rep from * across, ending with
ch 1, sc in 3rd ch of turning ch-3, ch 3, cl
in same ch-3 sp, turn. (29 3-dc groups)

Row 3: Rep Row 2, fasten off, turn.

Row 4: Attach white with a sl st in top
of cl, rep Row 2.

Row 5: Rep Row 3.

Row 6: With green, rep Row 4.

Rows 7 & 8: Rep Rows 2 and 3.

Rows 9 & 10: Rep Rows 4 and 5.

Row 11: With red, rep Row 4.

Rows 12–13: Rep Rows 2 and 3.

Rows 14–43: Rep Rows 4–13 alternately; at end of Row 43, fasten off.

Finishing

Cut 6 (12") lengths of red. Hold 2
strands tog and fold in half. Insert hook
from WS to RS behind end st of first
row on either short end of afghan, draw
folded end of strands through to form a
lp, draw free ends through lp, pull to
tighten. Rep for next 2 row ends, using
2 strands for each row. Matching color
of yarn to color of rows being worked,
rep for each rem row across same edge.
Rep across opposite short edge. ❖

Holiday Stripes & Baubles

Design by Katherine Eng

After the gifts are wrapped and under the tree, cuddle up with your sweetie in this colorful Christmas afghan!

Skill Level

Intermediate

Size

Approximately 40" x 55" excluding fringe

Materials

- Worsted weight yarn: 19 oz variegated (A), 17 oz burgundy (B), and 14 oz white (C)
- Size K/10½ crochet hook or size needed to obtain gauge

Gauge

[2 dc, ch 1, 2 dc] in pattern st = 2" with 2 strands held tog

Check gauge to save time.

Pattern Notes

Afghan is worked vertically from center to each side with 2 strands held tog throughout.

Leave 8" length for fringe at beg and end of each row when attaching new colors and fastening off colors not in use.

Pattern Stitch

Popcorn (pc): 4 dc in indicated sp or st, remove hook from lp, insert hook from RS to WS in top of first of last 4 dc made, pick up dropped lp, draw through st on hook.

First Half

Row 1 (RS): With 1 strand A and 1 strand B held tog, ch 157 (foundation ch), ch 3 more (turning ch-3), dc in 4th ch from hook, [ch 1, sk 2 chs, 2 dc in next ch] rep across, ch-1, turn. (53 pairs of dc, counting turning ch-3 as first dc)

Row 2: Sc in first dc, ch 1, sk next dc, sc in next ch-1 sp, [ch 2, sk 2 dc, sc in next ch-1 sp] rep across to last ch-1 sp, ch 1, sk next dc, sc in 3rd ch of turning ch-3, fasten off.

Row 3: With RS facing, attach 2 strands C held tog with a sl st in first ch-1 sp, ch 3 (counts as first dc throughout), dc in same sp, [ch 1, sk next sc, 2 dc in next ch-2 sp] rep across to last ch-2 sp, ch 1, sk next sc, 2 dc in last ch-1 sp, fasten off. (106 dc)

Row 4: With WS facing, attach 1 strand A and 1 strand B held tog with a sl st in first dc, ch 1, beg in first dc, rep Row 2 across, do not fasten off at end of row; turn.

Row 5: Sl st in first ch-1 sp, rep Row 3; do not fasten off at end of row; ch 1, turn.

Continued on page 139

CHAPTER 7

Candy Cane Throw

Continued from page 122

Rnd 5: With RS facing, attach 1 strand red and 1 strand white held tog with a sl st in first end ch-3 sp to the right at either end of panel, ch 3, [dc, ch 2, 2 dc] in same sp, *dc in each of next 7 sts, [2 dc, ch 2, 2 dc] in next sp, ch 1, sk next st, [fpdc over next st, ch 1,

sk next st] 57 times**, [2 dc, ch 2, 2 dc] in next sp, rep from * around, ending last rep at **, join in 3rd ch of beg ch-3, fasten off.

Rnd 6: With RS facing, attach 2 strands green held tog with a sl st in first end ch-2 sp to the right at either end of panel, ch 1, beg in same sp, *[2 sc, ch 3, 2 sc] in ch-2 sp, sk next st, sc in each of next 9 sts, [2 sc, ch 3, 2 sc] in next sp, sk next st, sc in next st, [working behind ch-1 sp, dc in next sk st of rnd before last, sc in next st] 58 times, rep from * around, join in beg sc.

Rnd 7: Sl st in next st, ch 1, sc in same st, *[sc, ch 3, sc] in next sp, sc in next st, [ch 3, sk next st, sc in next st] 6 times, [sc, ch 3, sc] in next sp, sc in next st, [ch 3, sk next st, sc in next st] 60 times, rep from * around, ending with ch 3, join in beg sc, fasten off. (136 ch-3 sps)

Rem 4 Panels

Rnds 1–6: Rep Rnds 1–6 for first panel.

Rnd 7: Sl st in next st, ch 1, sc in same st, [sc, ch 3, sc] in next sp, sc in next st,

[ch 3, sk next st, sc in next st] 6 times, [sc, jsp, sc] in next sp, sc in next st, [jsp, sk next st on working panel, sc in next st] 60 times, [sc, jsp, sc] in next sp, sc in next st, continue around as for Rnd 7 of first panel.

Border

With RS facing, attach 2 strands green held tog with a sl st in corner sp at right-hand end of either short edge, ch 6 (counts as first dc, ch-3), dc in same sp, *3 hdc in next sp, [3 sc in next sp] 4 times, 3 hdc in next sp **, 3 dc in jsp between panels, rep from * across to next corner sp, ending last rep at **, [dc, ch 3, dc] in corner sp, 2 dc in each sp across long edge to next corner †, [dc, ch 3, dc] in corner sp, rep from * around, ending last rep at †, join in 3rd ch of beg ch-3, fasten off. ❖

Crochet Tip

When crocheting a foundation chain, use a hook one size larger than the project. This will prevent slight gathering at the bottom of your project.

Organization Counts

Many of us accumulate lots of scrap yarn, but when a pattern calls for an ounce of one color or half an ounce of another, how do we know how much we have? Place each color inside a sealable plastic bag and weigh it on a diet or postage scale, marking the amount on the outside of the bag with a felt-tip marker. When the time comes to start your project, you'll know if you have enough of the required colors to complete your project.

— Ruth G. Shepherd

Easy Counting

When working a starting chain, an easy way to keep track of your stitch count is by using a bobby pin, safety pin or scrap of contrasting yarn to mark every 20th chain. If using yarn, pull yarn halfway through chain and tie a loose knot. If you lose track of your count, just count the markers rather than counting each chain from the beginning.

Make a longer starting chain than needed in case you lose count along the way. It's better to have too many than not enough. Extra chains can be undone or cut off if not needed.

— Isabelle Wolters

Keeping Your Place

Use a sticky note placed under the

row you are working on, and move it as you complete the row. This is especially helpful when working from a graph or chart.

If the pattern has several rows that are repeated throughout, write each row on a separate index card. Place in a pile and rotate the cards from top to bottom as you complete each row.

— Isabelle Wolters

Avoid Tangles

When working on an afghan that requires changing yarn colors many times in a single row, keep the yarns in a cardboard box. At the end of the row, turn the entire box instead of dealing with each skein. This will keep the yarn untwisted and tangle-free.

— Isabelle Wolters

Cranberry Ripple

Continued from page 132

Row 120: Attach B with a sl st in first sc, ch 4 (counts as first tr), *dc in next

sc, hdc in next sc, sc in next sc, sl st in ch-2 sp, sc in next sc, hdc in next sc, dc in next sc **, tr dec over next 2 sc, rep from * across to last st, ending last rep at **, tr in last st, fasten off.

Border

Rnd 1: With RS facing, attach C with a sl st at upper right-hand corner, ch 1, [sc, ch 2, sc] in same st, work 135 more sc evenly sp across last row to last st, [sc, ch 2, sc] in last st; *working over ends of rows across, work 191 more sc evenly sp across side to next corner *, [sc, ch 2, sc] in corner st, work 135 more sc across bottom to next corner, [sc, ch 2, sc] in corner st, rep from * to *, join in beg sc. (137 sc across each short edge; 193 sc across each long edge)

Rnd 2: Ch 3, dc in same st, *shell in corner sp, 2 dc in next sc, ch 1, sk 3 sts,

sc in next st, sk 3 sts, [shell in next st, sk 3 sts, sc in next st, sk 3 sts] rep across to next corner, ch 1 **, 2 dc in last sc before corner sp, rep from * around, ending last rep at **, join in 3rd ch of beg ch-3.

Rnd 3: Sl st in next dc, ch 1, sc in same st, =ch 1, sk next dc, sc in next dc, ch 1, [sc, ch 2, sc, ch 3, sc, ch 2, sc] in corner shell sp, ch 1, sk next dc, sc in next dc, *ch 1, sk next dc, sc in next dc, ch 1, sk next dc, sc in next sc, ch 1, sk next dc, sc in next dc **, ch 1, [sc, ch 3, sc] in shell sp, rep from * across to next corner, ending last rep at **, rep from † around, ending with ch 1, join in beg sc, fasten off. ❖

Holiday Stripes & Baubles

Continued from page 136

Row 6: Rep Row 2.

Row 7: With RS facing, attach 2 strands C held tog with a sl st in first ch-1 sp, ch 3, dc in same sp, ch 2, sk

next sc, pc in next ch-2 sp, [ch 3, sk next sc, dc in next ch-2 sp, ch 3, sk next sc, pc in next ch-2 sp] rep across to next-to-last ch-2 sp, ch 2, 2 dc in last ch-1 sp, fasten off.

Row 8: With WS facing, attach 1 strand A and 1 strand B held tog with a sl st in first dc, ch 1, sc in first dc, ch 1, sk next dc, sc in next sp, *ch 2, sk pc, sc in next sp **, ch 2, sk next dc, sc in next sp, rep from * across, ending last rep at **, ch 1, sc in 3rd ch of turning ch-3, turn.

Rows 9 & 10: Rep Rows 5 and 6.

Rows 11–13: Rep Rows 3–5.

Row 14: Rep Row 2 across; do not fasten off at end of row; ch 1, turn.

Row 15: Rep Row 5.

Row 16: Rep Row 2.

Rows 17–30: Rep Rows 3–16.

Rows 31 & 32: Rep Rows 3 and 4.

Row 33: Sc in first sp, [5 dc in next sp, sc in next sp] rep across, fasten off.

2nd Half

Row 1: With RS facing, attach 1 strand A and 1 strand B held tog with a sl st in first rem lp on opposite side of foundation ch at base of first pair of dc at right-hand edge, ch 3, dc in same st, [ch 1, 2 dc in rem lp at base of next pair of dc] rep across, ch 1, turn. (53 pairs of dc)

Rows 2–33: Rep Rows 2–33 of first half.

Fringe

Using 4 strands for each row that has a length of yarn rem from beg or ending a row and 5 strands for all other rows, cut 15" lengths of yarn to match color or row being worked. Holding all 4 or 5 strands tog, fold strands in half, insert hook from WS to RS through end st of first row across either short edge, draw folded end of strands through st to form a lp, draw free ends through lp and pull tightly to secure. Rep for each row across both short edges. ❖

Cozy Lap Afghans

*K*eep your legs cozy and warm with this collection of eight handsome afghans sized for your comfort and relaxation!

Chapter 8

Summertime Delight

Design by Sandra Abbate

*After just a couple days of crocheting,
you can be curled up with this cheery afghan
sipping a tall glass of lemonade!*

Pattern Notes

Join rnds with a sl st unless otherwise stated.

Afghan is worked from side to side holding 2 strands tog throughout.

To change color in sc, insert hook in indicated st, yo with working color, draw up a lp, drop working color to WS, yo with next color, complete sc.

Pattern Stitches

Small shell: [2 dc, ch 2, sc] in indicated sp or st.

Beg small shell: Ch 3, [dc, ch 2, sc] in first ch-2 sp.

Large shell: [4 dc, ch 3, 4 dc] in indicated sp or st.

Beg large shell: Ch 3, [3 dc, ch 3, 4 dc] in first ch-2 sp.

Afghan

Row 1 (WS): With yellow, ch 97 (foundation ch), ch 3 more (counts as first dc throughout), [dc, ch 2, sc] in 4th ch from hook (beg small shell made), [sk 2 chs, small shell in next ch] rep across, changing to blue in last st, turn. (33 small shells)

Skill Level

Intermediate

Size

40" x 50" including border

Materials

• Worsted weight yarn: 48 oz yellow and 24 oz blue
• Size N/15 crochet hook or size needed to obtain gauge

Gauge

2 small shells = 3" with 2 strands held tog

Check gauge to save time.

Row 2: Beg small shell, small shell in each rem ch-2 sp across, changing to yellow in last st, turn. (33 small shells)

Row 3: Rep Row 2, changing to blue in last st, turn.

Rows 4–47: Rep Rows and 3 alternately; at end of Row 47, do not change to blue in last st, do not fasten off; turn.

Border

Rnd 1: Beg large shell, [sc in next ch-2 sp, large shell in next ch-2 sp] 16 times, large shell over end st of same row, [sk next row, sc over end st of next row, sk next row, large shell over end st of next row] 11 times, large shell over end st of first row; working in rem lps of foundation ch at base of each small shell, sk beg small shell, [sc at base of next small shell, large shell at base of next small shell] 16 times, large shell over end st of Row 2, [sk next row, sc over

Continued on page 158

Rose Garden

Design by Michele Wilcox

If you enjoy flowers, then this charming afghan will be a delight to crochet and use throughout the year!

Pattern Notes

Join rnds with a sl st unless otherwise stated.

Afghan is worked with 2 strands held tog throughout.

Pattern Stitches

Shell: 5 dc in indicated st or sp.

Open shell: [{Dc, ch 1} twice, dc] in indicated st or sp.

Center Panel

Row 1 (RS): With gold, ch 20, [sc, hdc, dc] in 2nd ch from hook, [sk 2 chs, {sc, hdc, dc} in next ch] rep across to last 3 chs, sk 2 chs, sc in last ch, ch 1, turn. (19 sts)

Row 2: [Sc, hdc, dc] in first st, [sk next dc and next hdc, {sc, hdc, dc} in next sc] rep across to last 3 sts, sk last dc and last hdc, sc in last sc, ch 1, turn. (19 sts)

Rows 3–87: Rep Row 2; at end of Row 87, fasten off.

Inner Panel (make 2)

Row 1 (RS): With white, ch 16 (foundation ch), ch 3 more (turning ch-3), dc in 4th ch from hook, [ch 3, sk 3 chs, dc in each of next 2 chs, rep across, turn. (3 ch-3 sps)

Row 2: Ch 3 (counts as first dc throughout), [shell in center ch of next ch-3 sp] rep across, ending with dc in 3rd ch of turning ch-3, turn. (3 shells)

Row 3: Ch 3, dc in first dc of next

Skill Level

Intermediate

Size

38" x 48"

Materials

- Worsted weight yarn: 14 oz each gold and white, 11 oz green, and 2 oz pink
- Size K/10½ crochet hook or size needed to obtain gauge
- Tapestry needle

Gauge

3 shells = 5¼" with 2 strands held tog

Check gauge to save time.

shell, [ch 3, dc in last dc of same shell, dc in first dc of next shell] rep across, ending with ch 3, dc in last dc of last shell, dc in 3rd ch of turning ch-3, turn.

Rows 4–51: Rep Rows 2 and 3 alternately; at end of Row 51, fasten off.

Outer Panel (make 2)

Row 1 (RS): With green, ch 22, sc in 2nd ch from hook, *sk 2 chs, open shell in next ch, sk 2 chs, sc in next ch **, ch 3, sc in next ch, rep from * across, ending last rep at **, turn. (3 open shells)

Row 2: Ch 7 (counts as first tr, ch-3), *[sc, ch 3, sc] in center dc of next open shell, ch 3 **, dc in next ch-3 sp, ch 3, rep from * across, ending last rep at **, dc in last sc, ch 1, turn.

Row 3: Sc in first st, *sk next ch-3 sp,

open shell in next ch-3 sp**, sk next ch-3 sp, {sc, ch 3, sc} in next dc, rep from * across, ending last rep at **, sc in 4th ch of turning ch-7, ch 1, turn.

Rows 4–59: Rep Rows 2 and 3 alternately; at end of Row 59, fasten off.

Assembly

With tapestry needle, using photo as a guide, sew 1 inner panel along each side of center panel. Sew 1 outer panel along each inner panel.

Finishing
Edging

Rnd 1: With RS facing, attach green with a sl st in any corner, ch 1, 3 sc in same st, sc evenly sp around entire afghan, working 3 sc in each corner, join in beg sc, fasten off.

Rnd 2: With RS facing, attach white with a sl st in first of any 3 corner sc, ch 1, sc in same st, *[ch 3, sc in next st] twice, sk 2 sts, shell in next st, sk 2 sts, sc in next st, rep from * around, adjusting number of sts sk at end of rnd, if necessary, to end with shell in next st, join in beg sc, fasten off.

Rose (make 8)

Row 1: With pink, ch 14, 2 dc in 4th ch from hook, [ch 1, sc in next ch, ch 1, 3 dc in next ch] rep across, fasten off.

Roll Row 1 into rose shape. With tapestry needle and pink, sew bottom tog.

Leaf (make 8)

With green, ch 4, 9 dc in 4th ch from hook, join with sl st in 4th ch of ch-4, fasten off.

Using photo as a guide, sew 4 roses with leaves evenly sp down each white panel. ❖

Colors of Nature

Design by Dot Drake

*Rich natural shades come together to create
an attractive, touch-of-outdoors afghan
you're sure to enjoy!*

Pattern Notes

Join rnds with a sl st unless otherwise
stated.

Afghan is worked from side to side.

Pattern Stitch

V-st: [Dc, ch 2, dc] in indicated st or sp.

Afghan

Row 1 (WS): With tan, ch 183, sc in
2nd ch from hook and in each rem ch
across, turn. (182 sc)

Row 2: Ch 3 (counts as first dc
throughout), sk next st, V-st in next st,
[sk 2 sts, V-st in next st] rep across to
last 2 sts, sk next st, dc in next st, fasten off, turn. (60 V-sts)

Row 3: With WS facing, attach rose
with a sl st in first dc, ch 3, 3 dc in each
V-st sp across, dc in 3rd ch of turning
ch-3, turn.

Row 4: Ch 3, V-st in center dc of each
3-dc group across, dc in 3rd ch of turning ch-3, fasten off, turn. (60 V-sts)

Rows 5 & 6: With spruce green, rep
Rows 3 and 4.

Row 7: With WS facing, attach tan
with a sl st in first dc, ch 1, sc in same
st, 3 sc in each V-st sp across, sc in 3rd
ch of turning ch-3, ch 1, turn. (182 sc)

Row 8: Sc in each sc across, fasten off,
turn. (182 sc)

Row 9: With WS facing, attach rose in
first sc, ch 4 (counts as first dc, ch-1
throughout), [sk next unworked st, dc

Skill Level

Intermediate

Size

35" x 58"

Materials

- Worsted weight yarn: 8 oz
  spruce green, 6 oz rose, and 5
  oz tan
- Size I/9 crochet hook or size
  needed to obtain gauge

Gauge

16 sc = 5"

Check gauge to save time.

in each of next 3 sts, sc in sk st, drawing up sc to top of working row so work
does not pucker, ch 1] rep across to last
st, dc in last sc, turn.

Row 10: Ch 4, [sk sc, dc in each of
next 3 dc, sc in sk sc, drawing up sc to
top of working row so work does not
pucker, ch 1] rep across, ending with sk
4th ch of turning ch-4, dc in next ch,
fasten off.

Row 11: With WS facing, attach tan
with a sl st in first dc, ch 1, sc in same st,
sc in each rem sc and dc across, sc in 3rd
ch of turning ch-4, ch 1, turn. (182 sc)

Row 12: Rep Row 8.

Row 13: With WS facing, attach
spruce green with a sl st in first sc, rep
Row 2, do not fasten off; turn.

Row 14: Ch 3, 3 dc in each V-st sp
across, dc in 3rd ch of turning ch-3, fasten off. (182 dc)

Row 15: With WS facing, attach rose

with a sl st in first dc, rep Row 4; do
not fasten off; turn.

Row 16: Rep Row 14.

Row 17: With WS facing, attach tan
with a sl st in first st, ch 1, sc in same
st, sc in each rem dc across, sc in 3rd ch
of turning ch-3, ch 1, turn. (182 sc)

Row 18: Rep Row 8.

Rows 19 & 20: With spruce green,
rep Rows 9 and 10.

Rows 21 & 22: Rep Rows 11 and 12.

Rows 23 & 24: With rose, rep Rows
13 and 14.

Rows 25 & 26: With spruce green,
rep Rows 15 and 16.

Rows 27 & 28: Rep Rows 17 and 18.

Rows 29–48: Rep Rows 9–28.

Rows 49–66: Rep Rows 9–26.

Row 67: With tan, rep Row 15.

Row 68: Ch 2 (counts as first hdc), 3
hdc in each V-st sp across, hdc in 3rd
ch of turning ch-3, fasten off.

Border

With RS facing, attach spruce green
with a sl st at upper right corner, ch 1,
sc in same st, ch 3, sl st in 3rd ch from
hook, [sc in each of next 2 sts, ch 2, sl
st in 2nd ch from hook] rep across to
next corner, *[sc, ch 3, sl st in 3rd ch
from hook] in corner st; working 2 sc
over end st of each dc row and 1 sc over
end st of each sc row, continue in established pattern across to next corner *,
[sc, ch 3, sl st in 3rd ch from hook] in
corner st; working in rem lps of foundation ch, continue in established pattern across to next corner, rep from *
to *, join in beg sc, fasten off. ❖

Quick Squares

Design by Michele Wilcox

Use up oodles of scrap yarn with this handsome lap afghan worked in easy square motifs!

Pattern Notes

Join rnds with a sl st unless otherwise stated.

Afghan is worked with 2 strands held tog throughout.

Pattern Stitch

Picot (p): Ch 3, sc in 3rd ch from hook.

Square (make 1 of each color except white)

Row 1 (RS): Ch 30 (foundation ch), ch 3 more (turning ch-3), dc in 4th ch from hook, dc in each rem ch across, ch 1, turn. (31 dc, counting turning ch-3 as first dc)

Row 2: [Sc, 2 dc] in first st, [sk 2 sts, {sc, 2 dc} in next st] rep across to last 3 sts, sk 2 sts, sc in 3rd ch of turning ch-3, turn.

Row 3: Ch 3 (counts as first dc throughout), dc in each rem st across, ch 1, turn. (31 dc)

Skill Level

Intermediate

Size

Approximately 38" x 44" including border

Materials

- Bernat Berella "4" worsted weight yarn by Spinrite (3.5 oz per skein): 2 skeins each white #8942, medium gold #8811, light tapestry gold #8886, pale tapestry gold #8887, china rose #8923, medium navy #8838, pale antique rose #8814, medium ocean # 8762, light ocean #8761, and medium antique rose #8816
- Size K/10½ crochet hook or size needed to obtain gauge
- Tapestry needle

Gauge

[Sc, 2 dc] in pattern st = 1½" with 2 strands held tog

Check gauge to save time.

Rows 4–19: Rep Rows 2 and 3 alternately; at end of Row 19, ch 1, do not turn.

Edging

*Working over row ends, work 38 sc evenly sp to next corner *; working in rem lps across opposite side of foundation ch, 3 sc in first st, sc in each of next 29 rem lps, 3 sc in last st, rep from * to *, 3 sc in first st of last row of square, sc in each rem st across to last st, 3 sc in last st, join in beg sc, fasten off.

Assembly

Using photo as a guide, sew squares tog with tapestry needle in 3 rows of 3 squares each.

Border

Rnd 1: With RS facing, attach white with a sl st in any corner, ch 1, 3 sc in corner st, sc around, working 3 sc in each corner st, join in beg sc.

Rnd 2: Ch 1, sc in same st as joining, [sk 2 sc, 5 dc in next sc, sk 2 sc, sc in next st, p, sc in next st] rep around, adjusting number of sts sk at end of rnd if necessary to end with sc in last st, p, join in beg sc, fasten off. ❖

Embellish a Plain Afghan

To jazz up a plain afghan, crochet or embroider flowers, bows or other adornments and stitch randomly over the afghan. You can use up scraps of novelty yarns and those twisted with metallic filament; however, be sure the care properties are the same (machine washable and dryable).

Two-tone flower: Outer circle: Make a chain 6" long (or experiment with length). Dc in 4th ch from hook,

dc in each ch across. Fasten off, leaving an 8" length. With tapestry needle, weave end through sts of last row and pull tightly to gather into a circle. Tack first and last sts together.

Embroidered flower: Thread tapestry needle with 2–3 strands of yarn. Working with these strands doubled, embroider French knots where desired, wrapping yarn once around needle. For leaves, use doubled green yarn to embroider a straight stitch for each leaf.

Small bow: Ch 9 (experiment with one or two strands and number of chains depending on width of bow you want). Dc in 4th ch from hook. For large bow, work 5 rows (or number of rows desired, depending on weight of yarn). Fasten off. Finishing: Tightly wrap another strand of yarn a few times around center of bow. Sew or tie to afghan.

— Isabelle Wolters

Classic Cameo

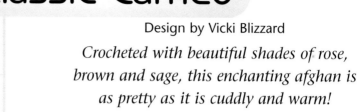

Design by Vicki Blizzard

*Crocheted with beautiful shades of rose,
brown and sage, this enchanting afghan is
as pretty as it is cuddly and warm!*

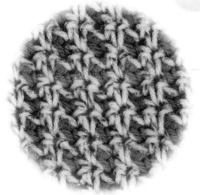

Pattern Note

Join rnds with a sl st unless otherwise stated.

Pattern Stitch

Lsc: Sc in next sk st of row before last, drawing st up to height of working row.

Afghan

Row 1 (RS): With MC, ch 102, sc in 2nd ch from hook and in each rem ch across, fasten off, turn. (101 sc)

Row 2: Attach C with a sl st in first sc, ch 1, sc in same st, [ch 1, sk next st, sc in next st] rep across, fasten off, turn. (51 sc, 50 ch-1 sps)

Row 3: Attach MC with a sl st in first st, ch 1, sc in same st, [lsc, sc in next st] rep across, fasten off, turn.

Row 4: With A, rep Row 2.

Row 5: Rep Row 3.

Row 6: With B, rep Row 2.

Row 7: Rep Row 3.

Rep Rows 2–7 until afghan measures approximately 41" from beg, ending with a Row 3, fasten off at end of last row.

Border

Rnd 1: With RS facing, attach MC with a sl st at upper right corner st, ch 1, 3 sc in same st, sc across to next cor-

Skill Level

Intermediate

Size

35" x 43" including border

Materials

- Coats & Clark Red Heart Fiesta worsted weight yarn (3.5 oz per skein): 3 skeins #6316 soft white (MC)
- Coats & Clark Red Heart Classic worsted weight yarn (3.5 oz per skein): 1 skein each cameo rose #759 (A), warm brown #336 (B) and medium sage #632 (C)
- Size K/10½ crochet hook or size needed to obtain gauge

Gauge

3 sc = 1"

Check gauge to save time.

ner, 3 sc in corner st; *working over row ends, sc evenly sp across to next corner *, 3 sc in corner st, sc in each rem lp across opposite side of foundation ch to next corner, 3 sc in corner st, rep from * to *, join in beg sc, ch 1, turn.

Rnd 2: Sc in each sc around, working 3 sc in each corner st, join in beg sc, ch 1, turn.

Rnd 3: Rep Rnd 2; do not ch 1; fasten off. ❖

Easy Fringe

When working on an afghan that has rows of different colors, eliminate the tedious job of weaving in ends. Make "fringe as you go" instead, and eliminate the edging. When changing colors, leave a 6" length of yarn at the beginning and end of the row where the color change takes place. These ends can be combined with extra fringe worked after the afghan is finished. Fringe will be either at sides or top and bottom of afghan, depending on which direction the afghan is worked.

— Isabelle Wolters

Avoid Those Holes

When working motifs which begin with a chain joined into a ring, if you don't like the appearance of a hole at the beginning of the round, leave a 4"–6" length of yarn at the beginning and work your stitches over it while working into the ring. At the end of the round, pull the end tightly to close the hole. This will keep the centers of all your motifs consistent.

A second method is to begin with ch-2 instead of the ring if the pattern begins with sc. Work the required sc into the 2nd ch from the hook, using it as the ring. If the pattern begins with dc in the ring, begin with ch-4 instead of the ring and work the required dc in the 4th chain from the hook, using it as the ring.

— Isabelle Wolters

Lilac Blossoms

Design by Laura Gebhardt

Capture the essence of spring's most beautiful lilac bush with this exquisite afghan!

Skill Level

Intermediate

Size

Approximately 34" x 45" including border

Materials

• Worsted weight yarn: 22 oz lilac
• Size H/8 crochet hook or size needed to obtain gauge

Gauge

2 shells = 2½"

Check gauge to save time.

Pattern Note

Join rnds with a sl st unless otherwise stated.

Pattern Stitches

Cl: Holding back on hook last lp of each st, 2 dc in indicated st or sp, yo, draw through all 3 lps on hook.

Shell: [{Cl, ch 2} twice, cl] in indicated st or sp.

Picot (p): Ch 3, sl st in 3rd ch from hook.

P cl: Holding back on hook last lp of each st, 3 dc in indicated st or sp, yo, draw through all 4 lps on hook, p.

Afghan

Row 1 (RS): Ch 131 (foundation ch), ch 5 more (turning ch-5; counts as first dc, ch-2), cl in 6th ch from hook, [sk 4 chs, shell in next ch] rep across to last 5 chs, sk 4 chs, [cl, ch 2, dc] in last ch, ch 1, turn. (25 shells)

Row 2: Sc in first dc, [ch 4, sc in center cl of next shell] rep across, ending with ch 4, sc in 3rd ch of turning ch-5, turn. (26 ch-4 sps)

Row 3: Ch 5 (counts as first dc, ch-2), cl in first sc, shell in each sc across to last sc, [ch, ch 2, dc] in last sc, ch 1, turn. (25 shells)

Rows 4–84: Rep Rows 2 and 3 alternately, ending with a Row 2; at end of Row 84, turn.

Border

Rnd 1: Sl st in first sc and in each of next 2 chs of first ch-4 sp, ch 1, sc in same ch-4 sp, *[ch 4, sc in next ch-4 sp] 25 times, ch 7, sc over end st of next shell row (corner made), [ch 5, sk next row, sc over end st of next shell row] 41 times; working across opposite side of foundation ch, ch 7 *, sc in first ch-4 sp (corner made), rep from * to *, join in beg sc.

Rnd 2: Sl st in each of first 2 chs of first ch-5 sp, ch 1, sc in same sp, *ch 3, [p cl, ch 3] 3 times in next sp, sc in next sp, rep from * across to corner sp, ch 3, [p cl, ch 3] 4 times in corner sp**, sc in next sp, rep from * around, ending last rep at **, join in beg sc, fasten off. ❖

Chunky Shells

Design by Katherine Eng

*Warm up by the fire in this warm and cozy afghan!
Worked with two strands held together,
it will crochet up quickly and easily.*

Pattern Notes

Join rnds with a sl st unless otherwise stated.

Afghan is worked with 1 strand of each color held tog throughout.

Pattern Stitches

Shell: [3 dc, ch 2, 3 dc] in indicated st or sp.

Small p lp (sm p lp): Ch 8, sl st in 8th ch from hook.

Large p lp (lg p lp): Ch 10, sl st in 10th ch from hook.

Corner p group: [Sl st, sm p lp, sl st, lg p lp, sl st, sm p lp, sl st] in corner st.

First Half

Row 1 (RS): Beg at center and working to side, ch 162, sc in 2nd ch from hook, [ch 3, sk 3 chs, sc in next ch] rep across, ch 1, turn. (40 ch-3 sps)

Row 2: Sc in first sc, [ch 3, sk 3 chs, sc in next sc] rep across, ch 1, turn.

Row 3: Sc in first sc, [sk 3 chs, shell in next sc, sk 3 chs, sc in next sc] rep

Skill Level

Intermediate

Size

42" x 56" including border

Materials

- Worsted weight yarn: 22 oz each lavender and spruce green
- Size N/15 crochet hook or size needed to obtain gauge

Gauge

Shell = 2½" with 2 strands held tog

Check gauge to save time.

across, turn. (20 shells)

Row 4: Ch 3 (counts as first dc throughout), dc in first sc, ch 2, sc in shell sp, [ch 3, dc in next sc, ch 3, sc in next shell sp] rep across to last shell sp, ch 2, 2 dc in last sc, ch 1, turn.

Row 5: Sc in first dc, ch 3, sc in next sc, [ch 3, sk 3 chs, sc in next dc, ch 3, sk 3 chs, sc in next sc] rep across to last sc, ch 3, sk next ch-2 sp and next dc, sc in 3rd ch of turning ch-3, ch 1, turn.

Row 6: Rep Row 2.

Rows 7–34: Rep Rows 3–6 alternately; at end of Row 34, fasten off.

2nd Half

Row 1: With RS facing, attach yarn with sl st in first rem lp of foundation ch on first half at base of first sc, ch 1, sc in same st, [ch 3, sc in rem lp at base of next sc] rep across, ch 1, turn. (40 ch-3 sps)

Rows 2–34: Rep Rows 2–34 of first half; at end of Row 34, do not ch 1; turn.

Border

Rnd 1: Corner p group in first sc, *ch 1, [sl st, sm p lp, sl st] in next ch-3 sp, ch 1 **, [sl st, sm p lp, sl st] in next sc, rep from * across to next corner sc, ending last rep at **, corner p group in corner sc, ch 1; working over ends of rows across, counting end st of each sc row as 1 st, top of each dc or turning ch-3 as 1 st, and post of each dc or turning ch-3 as 1 st, [sk next st, {sl st, sm p lp, sl st} in next st, ch 1] rep across to next corner st, corner p group in corner st, rep from * around, ending with ch 1, join in beg sl st, fasten off. ❖

Shells & Diamonds

Design by Vicki Blizzard

Select your favorite colors and work them together into this enchanting lap afghan rich with texture and style!

Pattern Note

Join rnds with a sl st unless otherwise stated.

Pattern Stitch

Shell: 5 dc in indicated st.

Afghan

Row 1 (RS): Ch 110 (foundation ch), ch 3 more (turning ch-3), dc in 4th ch from hook and in each rem ch across, turn. (111 dc, counting turning ch-3 as first dc)

Row 2: Ch 3 (counts as first dc throughout), dc in each of next 2 sts, *sk 2 sts, shell in next st, ch 2, sk 3 sts **, dc in each of next 5 sts, rep from * across to last 3 sts, ending last rep at **, dc in each of next 2 dc, dc in 3rd ch of turning ch-3, turn. (10 shells)

Row 3: Ch 3, dc in each of next 2 dc, *shell in first dc of next shell, ch 2 **, dc in each of next 2 dc, ch 1, sk next dc, dc in each of next 2 dc, rep from * across to last shell, ending last rep at **, sk 4 dc, dc in each of next 2 dc, dc in

Experience Level

Intermediate

Size

Approximately 33 x 45 inches including border

Materials

- Lion Brand Imagine mohair-like worsted weight yarn (2 oz per skein): 6 balls each strawberry fields #303
- Size J/10 crochet hook or size needed to obtain gauge

Gauge

18 dc = 5"

Check gauge to save time.

3rd ch of turning ch-3, turn. (10 shells)

Row 4: Ch 3, dc in each of next 2 dc, *sk next ch-2 sp, shell in first dc of next shell, ch 2 **, [dc in next dc, ch 1, sk next dc, dc in next dc] twice, ch 1, sk next dc, dc in next dc, rep from * across to last shell, ending last rep at **, sk 4 dc, dc in each of next 2 dc, dc in 3rd ch of turning ch-3, turn.

Row 5: Rep Row 3.

Row 6: Ch 3, dc in each of next 2 dc, *shell in first dc of next shell, ch 2 **, sk 3 dc, dc in each of next 5 dc, rep from * across to last shell, ending last rep at **, dc in each of next 2 dc, dc in 3rd ch of turning ch-3, turn.

Rows 7–62: Rep Rows 3–6 alternately.

Row 63: Ch 3, dc in each of next 2 dc, *sk next sp, hdc in next dc, sc in each of next 3 dc, hdc in next dc **, dc in each of next 5 dc, rep from * across to last shell, ending last rep at **, dc in each of next 2 dc, dc in 3rd ch of turning ch-3, ch 1, turn.

Border

Rnd 1: 2 sc in first st, sc in each rem st across to next corner, 3 sc in last st; *working over row ends, 3 sc over end st of each row across to next corner, 3 sc in corner st, sc in each rem lp across opposite side of foundation ch to next corner, 3 sc in last st, rep from * to *, sc in same st as beg sc, join in beg sc, ch 1, turn.

Rnd 2: With RS facing, sc in same st as joining, [sk 2 sc, shell in next sc, sk 2 sc, sc in next sc] rep around, adjusting number of sts sk at end of rnd if necessary so pattern rep will come out even, join in beg sc, fasten off. ❖

Summertime Delight

Continued from page 142

end st of next row, sk next row, large shell over end st of next row] rep across, join in 3rd ch of beg ch-3.

Rnd 2: Ch 1, sc in same st as joining, *sc in each dc and [sc, ch 3, sc] in each ch-3 sp around, join in beg sc, fasten off. ❖

Special Thanks

Location for chapter 3 intro- duction courtesy of Geneva Lions Club, Geneva, Ind.

Location courtesy of Oubache State Park, Ind.

Location courtesy of Swiss Heritage Village, Berne, Ind.

Buyer's Guide

To find materials listed, first check your local yarn, craft and fabric stores. If you are unable to locate a product locally, contact the following manufacturers for their products.

- **Caron International**
  1550 Shepphard Mill Rd.
  Greenville, SC 27834
  (800) 444-2284

- **Coats & Clark**
  Consumer Service
  P.O. Box 12229
  Greenville, SC 26912-0229
  (800) 648-1479

- **Lion Brand Yarns**
  34 W. 15th St.
  New York, NY 10011
  (800) 795-5466

- **Patons**
  Consumer Service
  1001 Roselawn Ave.
  Toronto, Ontario M6B 1B8
  Canada
  (800) 268-3620

- **Spinrite Yarns**
  P.O. Box 40
  Listowel, Ontario N4W 3H3
  Canada
  (519) 291-3780
  USA
  P.O. Box 435
  Lockport, NY 14094-6435
  (800) 265-2864

General Instructions

Please review the following information before working the patterns in this book. Important details about the abbreviations and symbols used and finishing instructions are included.

HOOKS

Crochet hooks are sized for different weights of yarn and thread. Keep in mind that the sizes given with the pattern instructions were obtained by working with the size yarn and hook given in the materials list. If you work with a smaller hook, depending on your gauge, your project size will be smaller; if you work with a larger hook, your finished project's size will be larger.

GAUGE

Gauge is determined by the tightness or loose-ness of your stitches, and affects the finished size of your project. If you are concerned about the finished size of the project matching the size given, take time to crochet a small section of the pattern and then check your gauge. For example, if the gauge called for is 10 dc = 1 inch, and your gauge is 12 dc to the inch, you should switch to a larger hook. On the other hand, if your gauge is only 8 dc to the inch, you should switch to a smaller hook.

If the gauge given in the pattern is for an entire motif, work one motif and then check your gauge.

UNDERSTANDING SYMBOLS

As you work through a pattern, you'll quickly notice several symbols in the instructions. These symbols are used to clarify the pattern for you: Brackets [], curlicue brackets {}, asterisks *.

Brackets [] are used to set off a group of instructions worked a number of times. For example, "[ch 3, sc in ch-3 sp] 7 times" means to work the instructions inside the [] seven times. Brackets [] also set off a group of stitches to be worked in one stitch, space or loop. For example, the brackets [] in this set of instructions, "Sk 3 sc, [3 dc, ch 1, 3 dc] in next st" indicate that after skipping 3 sc, you will work 3 dc, ch 1 and 3 more dc all in the next stitch.

Occasionally, a set of instructions inside a set of brackets needs to be repeated too. In this case, the text within the brackets to be repeated will be set off with curlicue brackets {}. For example, "[Ch 9, yo twice, insert hook in 7th ch from hook and pull up a loop, sk next dc, yo, insert hook in next dc and pull up a loop, {yo and draw through 2 lps on hook} 5 times, ch 3] 8 times." In this case, in each of the eight times you work the instructions included in brackets, you will work the section included in curlicue brackets five times.

Asterisks * are also used when a group of instructions is repeated. They may either be used alone or with brackets. For example, "*Sc in each of the next 5 sc, 2 sc in next sc, rep from * around, join with a sl st in beg sc" simply means you will work the instructions from the first * around the entire round.

"*Sk 3 sc, [3 dc, ch 1, 3 dc] in next st, rep from * around" is an example of asterisks working with brackets. In this set of instructions, you will repeat the instructions from the asterisk around, working the instructions inside the brackets together.

STITCH ABBREVIATIONS

beg	begin(ning)
bl(s)	block(s)
bpdc	back post dc
ch(s)	chain(s)
cl(s)	cluster(s)
CC	contrasting color
dc	double crochet
dec	decrease
dtr	double treble crochet
fpdc	front post dc
hdc	half-double crochet
inc	increase
lp(s)	loop(s)
MC	main color
meas	measure(s)
p	picot
rem	remain(ing)
rep	repeat
rnd(s)	round(s)
RS	right side
sc	single crochet
sk	skip
sl st	slip stitch
sp(s)	space(s)
st(s)	stitch(es)
tog	together
tr	treble crochet
trtr	triple treble crochet
WS	wrong side
yo	yarn over

STITCH GUIDE

Front Loop (a) Back Loop (b)

Chain (ch)
Yo, draw lp through hook.

Slip Stitch Joining
Insert hook in beg ch, yo, draw lp through.

Front Post/Back Post Dc
Fpdc (a): Yo, insert hook from front to back and to front again around the vertical post (upright part) of next st, yo and draw yarn through, yo and complete dc.
Bpdc (b): Yo, reaching over top of piece and working on opposite side (back) of work, insert hook from back to front to back again around vertical post of next st, yo and draw yarn through, yo and complete dc.

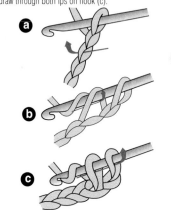

Single Crochet (sc)
Insert hook in st (a), yo, draw lp through (b), yo, draw through both lps on hook (c).

Half-Double Crochet (hdc)
Yo, insert hook in st (a), yo, draw lp through (b), yo, draw through all 3 lps on hook (c).

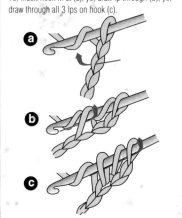

DECREASING

Single Crochet Decrease
Dec 1 sc over next 2 sts as follows: Draw up a lp in each of next 2 sts, yo, draw through all 3 lps on hook.

Double Crochet Decrease
Dec 1 dc over next 2 sts as follows: [Yo, insert hook in next st, yo, draw up lp on hook, yo, draw through 2 lps] twice, yo, draw through all 3 lps on hook.

Double Crochet (dc)
Yo, insert hook in st (a), yo, draw lp through (b), [yo, draw through 2 lps] twice (c, d).

Treble Crochet (tr)
Yo hook twice, insert hook in st (a), yo, draw lp through (b), [yo, draw through 2 lps on hook] 3 times (c, d, e).

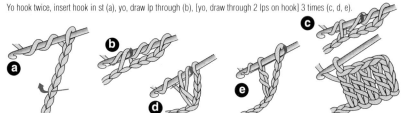

SPECIAL STITCHES

Chain Color Change (ch color change)
Yo with new color, draw through last lp on hook.

Double Crochet Color Change (dc color change)
Drop first color, yo with new color, draw through last 2 lps of st.

Reverse Single Crochet (reverse sc)
Working from left to right, insert hook in next st to the right (a), yo, draw up lp on hook, complete as for sc (b).

Stitch Abbreviations
The following stitch abbreviations are used throughout this publication.

beg	begin(ning)
bl(s)	block(s)
bpdc	back post dc
ch(s)	chain(s)
cl(s)	cluster(s)
CC	contrasting color
dc	double crochet
dec	decrease
dtr	double treble crochet
fpdc	front post dc
hdc	half-double crochet
inc	increase
lp(s)	loop(s)
MC	main color
p	picot
rem	remain(ing)
rep	repeat
rnd(s)	round(s)
RS	right side facing you
sc	single crochet
sk	skip
sl st	slip stitch
sp(s)	space(s)
st(s)	stitch(es)
tog	together
tr	treble crochet
trtr	triple treble crochet
WS	wrong side facing you
yo	yarn over

Crochet Hooks

METRIC	US
.60mm	14 steel
.75mm	12 steel
1.00mm	10 steel
1.25mm	8 steel
1.50mm	7 steel
1.75mm	5 steel
2.00mm	B/1
2.50mm	C/2
3.00mm	D/3
3.50mm	E/4
4.00mm	F/5
4.50mm	G/6
5.00mm	H/8
5.50mm	I/9
6.00mm	J/10

Yarn Conversion
OUNCES TO GRAMS

1	28.4
2	56.7
3	85.0
4	113.4

GRAMS TO OUNCES

25	⅞
40	1⅔
50	1¾
100	3½

Crochet Abbreviations

US	INTL
sc—single crochet	dc—double crochet
dc—double crochet	tr—treble crochet
hdc—half-double crochet	htr—half treble crochet
tr—treble crochet	dtr—double treble crochet
dtr—double treble crochet	trip—triple treble crochet
sk—skip	miss

YARNS
Bedspread weight	No. 10 cotton or Virtuoso
Sport weight	3-ply or thin DK
Worsted weight	Thick DK or Aran

Check tension or gauge to save time.